I0467934

Become
THE LEADER
Your
PEOPLE DESERVE

RICHARD BROWN

RICHARD BROWN

Copyright © 2014 Richard Brown

All rights reserved.

ISBN-13: 978-1500547875
ISBN-10: 1500547875

Printed in the United States of America

PRAISE FOR

Become **THE LEADER**
Your **PEOPLE DESERVE**

"I believe this is a good and useful resource for those getting ready to undertake a leadership role. It will help those just venturing into the unpredictable role of being a leader."

--Robert J Mursch
SMSgt, USAF (Ret.)

"This is a practical, eye opening explanation of the leadership process. This book is a valuable read for all in management."

--Larry Lermo
Richard Brown's first civilian boss

"This book addresses the core of superb management, i.e. day-to-day leadership. The stories are interesting and germane. It will be useful for all managers, but especially first and middle level managers who want to become successful leaders."

--B.J. Robison
Retired Executive Vice President of Sales

RICHARD BROWN

"A truly personal account of a journey that explores leadership in action. It's a reminder of how careers and life experiences are shaped by strong leaders."

--Meg VanderLaan
Corporate Communications Consultant

"This book provides very helpful information for the situation in which I find myself! I must accomplish the impossible without the resources, time or people. It looks like leadership is the way to go!"

--Andy Keith
Husband, Father and General Manager

"This book is a sure-fire catalyst to recognizing, inspiring and equipping dynamic and compassionate leaders."

--Connie Grosse
High School Teacher of 33 years

"I intend to share this book with my son. If I had only been exposed to this book earlier in my career, I could have been much more prepared to lead my region during my twenty-year tenure as the leader of a sales team."

--Charlie Rodgers
Retired Senior Regional Sales Manager

"To paraphrase Sir Winston Churchill. This is not the end, it is not even the beginning of the end, yet it is a useful beginning of the leadership experience. Keep learning, keep reading and keep looking for new experiences."

--Art Thurnauer
Principal at Leadership Development and Coaching

This book is dedicated to the memory of Colonel John W. Ripley, USMC

On April 2, 1972, Colonel John Ripley defined the concept of *commitment* by destroying a bridge over the Dong Ha River in the Republic of South Vietnam, halting a massive armored advance by the North Vietnamese Army, saving countless South Vietnamese and American lives and earning the Navy Cross for his actions.

Upon his return to the United States, he was posted as the Marine Option Instructor for the Naval R.O.T.C. program at Oregon State University. For the next three years, he taught the concepts of *leadership* to hundreds of midshipmen and prepared students to become Navy and Marine Corps officers (including the author of this book). Those midshipmen have gone on to pay it forward by leading in all aspects of Naval Service and in their respective lives following their military careers.

Colonel Ripley is a hero from the mold of other combat legends such as Chesty Puller, Alvin York and Hal Moore and his legacy will live forever in the annals of military history. Just as importantly, for the thousands of young men and women who had the good fortune to have "The Rip" cross their path, he became the "answer to the question" for them. (You will discover "the question" as you progress through this book.)

Semper Fi, Colonel! Thank you for all you have done for me, my shipmates and America! This is my effort in some small way to pay it forward.

Table of Contents

I must gratefully acknowledge the assistance of

Beth Rich Brown

in the creation of this book. For decades, she has been at my side while I faced challenges, frustrations and victories as I constructed my own *leadership* puzzle. She has listened to war stories swapped between myself and my friends while sharing small batch bourbon and vodka martinis. Her own experiences with both inspirational leaders, as well as with leaders unfamiliar with the skill they were expected to exhibit helped in opening my eyes to the need for this book. Thank you!

It would be inappropriate to neglect to mention all my family, friends, colleagues and former leaders as well that put their own brain power and elbow grease into making this book work. I would say that it could not have been written without them but that is incorrect. While without their assistance it certainly **would** have been written, it would have been virtually unreadable. Because of the selfless hours spent editing and proofreading on their parts, this mass of thoughts has become a book. The barrels of red ink sacrificed eliminating countless commas and the inappropriate use of the word "that" is awe inspiring. Thank you for your candor as well as for the 😊 and positive reinforcement within the margins. Those were the warm fuzzies I needed to keep me pounding away on the keyboard. I am very grateful I "friended up" as much as I have. I hope the finished product makes you proud!

MAKE THIS BOOK WORK FOR YOU

As the potential reader of this book (after all, you just started and it would be unwise to make any assumptions) I <u>am</u> going to make a supposition. If you are motivated enough to get past this introduction and into the depths of the chapters, you most likely fit one of two distinct profiles:

1.   You are an individual who fills a *leadership* role somewhere in your life. Whether as a manager at work, a coach, a teacher or a parent, the challenge of getting other people to accomplish objectives is a big part of what you do. Something about that experience has energized you and hopefully you have enjoyed the significant rewards that result from being a leader. In fulfilling that role, you have encountered a *leadership* challenge or two. You are looking for some guidance that will assist you in becoming more effective in your *leadership* position.

2.   You are an individual who is embarking upon your first *leadership* experience. It wouldn't be far off to guess that you are in your late teens or early twenties and someone has directed you to

this book. Regardless of your age, you are feeling proud of your recent appointment and a bit overwhelmed. Your first reaction may be to look over your shoulder and to follow the examples set by those who have led you in the past. (I can't say that is a poor approach as it worked out well for me!) You are now faced with two questions to answer. The first question will be discussed early in the "Foundations of *Leadership*" chapter.

The second question is: "Which of my examples from the past should I be following?" Regardless of which of the categories you find yourself, you can now rest a bit easier knowing that you have discovered a resource that will greatly assist you in successfully creating your own *leadership* experience.

This book was written to accomplish three things: to complement, to supplement and to distill.

Complement:

Even though many environs in which we find ourselves may suffer a serious *leadership* deficiency, there is NO such shortage of books on *leadership* or *leadership* theories. Search *"leadership"* and you will be treated to pages ad infinitum advertising *leadership* consultants. Professional Resource Enhancement (my organization, and as we affectionately refer to it: PRE will be one of them.) I don't pretend that I have all the answers, just as I know that nobody else does either.

Supplement:

Ironically, all the answers **do** exist out there somewhere. Do not expect to find them all at once. Like a "jigsaw puzzle", if you first observe what pieces are available, select the ones that relate to the area on which you are working and then join them, you will eventually begin to complete the image you seek. In this case, that would be a clear and progressively more complete picture of what it takes to be an effective and inspirational leader.

Distill:

I am confident that the pieces provided here will find a place in **your** puzzle. I also believe they will be more than just random, nondescript pieces that fit, but hold little practical value for image definition. The pieces you receive here are equivalent to the all-important four corner pieces that are the beginnings of any successful puzzle construction. You will also see before long that they do all fit together. It is my belief that *leadership* is not rocket science, brain surgery or advanced organic chemistry. There is no need to commit to memory twelve traits, fourteen principles, eighty secrets or an infinite number of tactics to be an effective leader. All you need to remember are the three fundamentals to any relationship which we will explore in depth. Conduct yourself according to those fundamentals as well as the foundation that they must be built upon and you will maximize your chances for success. With just a bit of analysis, every lesson in *leadership* can be distilled down to those four key core values.

It is my intention for this book to be more than just a one-time read from cover to cover and then serve the rest of its shelf life propping up two bookends. Neither is it designed to be lost amidst the 100's of volumes in your digital book shelf. Like the first teddy bear you received as a child, it is my hope that it will be well loved enough with notes, dog ears, page tabs and highlighters to occupy a place of honor on either a digital desktop or the actual desktop where you do your work.

Once you finish the section that is titled "The Foundations of *Leadership*" the remainders of the chapters are designed to be read as required. Facing a problem with too much to get done alone? Read the section "**Everything I Need to Know About *Trust, I Learned on Day One! (Almost)*"** in the *Trust* chapter. Do you have teammates who don't seem to be performing as well as you would have expected? There is a section titled **Small Batch Bourbon for My Horses** in the chapter on *Caring* that you will find useful, among others.

Throughout the book, you will find relevant examples of *leadership* from real life. The text describing these examples will be italicized. In most cases, the names have all been changed to "protect the innocent" but I assure you they have all occurred and are meant to relate to that chapter or section. If you are pushed for time and decide to skip the personal example, the chapter will still be useful to you, just not as much fun. Once you have read the meat of that chapter, you may wish to go back and enjoy the story regarding the issues that you have reviewed.

THINK OUTSIDE OF THE BOX

As you read this book, you will notice that I have chosen to focus my analogies on examples of *leadership* involving military leaders, educators, coaches and business managers. It is quite possible that your current field of endeavor is not related to any of those activities. That certainly does not mean that the examples within do not apply to you and any leadership challenge that you may face. It does mean that to get the most out of the information presented, it will be helpful for you to "think outside of the box." (That is not a bad trait for a leader in any case.)

You may not deal with issues of life and death, but the *leadership* skills displayed by a combat leader in a life or death situation differ from your challenges only by a matter of degrees. For too long, organizations have suffered under a debilitating form of ethnocentrism. Many organizations feel that lessons learned in other fields of endeavor have no relevance to their challenges. Perhaps that is true about technical matters, but *leadership* is not a technical matter, it is a people issue and people are people regardless of their profession.

ASSIST THOSE WHO HAVE PAID THE PRICE

Many of those who have served our nation in *leadership* positions during recent conflicts have paid a heavy price in the performance of their duties. It is inherent to the mission of PRE that our efforts provide support to organizations that seek to assist those heroes in recovering from their sacrifice. As a result, each year we will donate ten percent of the gross income from our books to a PRE-selected organization whose mission includes assisting those heroes in the memory of Colonel John W. Ripley, USMC.

BUYING THE BOOK

As the purchaser of this book, I encourage you to explore the premium website of Professional Resource Enhancement. (www.pre-leadership.com). On this site, you will find tools to further your *leadership* development. Profits from sales are nice and assisting our nation's heroes is important, but they aren't the primary purpose of what we do. What is more important are the number of leaders and future leaders who are reached with these concepts. In the event you wish to gift this book to someone once you complete it, I couldn't be happier! Should you decide to pass this book on to a protégé or peer, I would also ask that you consider making a monetary donation to an organization that PRE supports. Your gift of your copy of the book does reduce our income; but by gifting to our partner organization it does not impinge on our efforts to assist those charitable efforts.

PAYING IT FORWARD

While it is the responsibility of any team leader to provide guidance and support to their team for them to accomplish their objective, the leader of the team has the equally important responsibility of developing the people with whom they work. I want to encourage and facilitate this behavior. If you find my perspectives useful and know of someone embarking upon a *leadership* assignment with little or no previous *leadership* experience, please direct them to our website:

www.pre-leadership.com

Thank you for giving me a portion of your valuable time. It is my fervent desire that you will find the concepts conveyed within useful enough to make the investment in your *leadership* development productive.

THE FOUNDATIONS OF LEADERSHIP

"Whatever you leave behind is not engraved in stone monuments, but what is woven into the lives of others."

--Pericles

RICHARD BROWN

THE FOUNDATIONS OF LEADERSHIP

How would you like to amaze your friends and confuse your enemies? Perform this little parlor trick: open a jigsaw puzzle. The number of pieces in the puzzle doesn't matter. It can be a four-piece puzzle designed for a child or a thousand-piece puzzle depicting an Arctic blizzard in mid-winter. Now put the puzzle together without the aid of a table, floor or any other type of horizontal hard surface. Challenging to say the least, isn't it?

Picture *leadership* as a puzzle. Successful leaders could imagine the whole of their *leadership* experience as a puzzle that is close to completion. As effective leaders, they know that puzzle will never be completed, yet they strive to add more to the image. Over time, as they have acquired pieces of that puzzle in the form of various experiences, successes, failures, books read, seminars attended, and discussions participated in, growth of the image has taken place. Their image of *leadership* has become more complete and clear, piece by piece. As it is completed, it is important to realize that their image may be different from the image being constructed by another leader. Your image is **your** image. It doesn't need to be identical to the images of others. But before leaders can attempt to join the various pieces of their puzzles, they need to find a foundation on which to build. Within this chapter, you will find your foundation.

Leadership can be a richly rewarding endeavor and it can also be a tremendously frustrating experience. When you assume the mantle of *leadership*, for example as a business manager, a teacher or a coach, you accept a task that can be stressful, lonely and frustrating. Many of those who assume the role for the wrong reasons are quick to experience those feelings. The key here is "the wrong reasons." Before you make the decision to place yourself in "The *Leadership* Spotlight" you need to ask yourself a very important question as well as come up with a very solid answer:

"WHY DO I WANT TO LEAD?"

When one is standing in the ranks, or sitting in a cubicle, and looks at those in *leadership* positions, the visible trappings of *leadership* can be very seductive. Private offices (instead of adjacent desks with irritating colleagues), recognition, impressive titles, pay increases and power all can be very tempting to an entry or mid-level employee. Ironically, the more **in**effective previous leaders have been, the more likely it is that the potential *leadership* trainee has developed a false image of the true rewards of *leadership*. Effective and inspirational leaders do not make a habit of flaunting the privileges of their position. The ineffective leader has nothing more than perquisites with which to underscore their title to their colleagues. A leader who has been appointed, having never asked themselves the above question, may well be there for the wrong reasons. These individuals, unappreciative of the privileges of a position of *leadership* rarely understand, and frequently minimize, the true rewards that come from leading others. They prefer to make a visible demonstration of the material benefits of their position, particularly to those on the team they serve.

THE REWARDS OF *LEADERSHIP*

Baseballs weigh approximately five ounces with a circumference of about nine inches. In the major leagues an average of forty-six baseballs are used in every game. While their intrinsic value is minimal, like anything else, if you attach enough emotional significance to it, they can become priceless.

The phone rang and the voice on the other end was the Coach's son. It had been fifteen years since the Coach had done any coaching, but to the boys (now men) who were on the baseball team, he was still known as "Coach." He and his son spoke just about every day, so this call wasn't any big surprise, at least at first. It turns out that the Coach's son had a Visitor. Out of the blue, another member of their baseball team had tracked down the son and they were reconnecting. Soon after arriving, the Visitor asked if they could call Coach. Before you knew it, Coach was reconnecting with the Visitor as well. Shortly into the conversation, the Visitor related a story that repaid his Coach in full for all the days spent loading baseball gear into the car, constructing lineups, suffering through rainouts, and personally footing the bills for team baseball gear. The hours spent figuring batting averages, ERAs, and other baseball statistics from the most recent game tracing the development of his players and all the tasks that define coaching seemed like a small sacrifice.

When he was young, the Visitor rarely had the pleasure of having his father watch him play baseball. His dad worked hard to support his family. Dad's job prevented him from seeing most of his son's games. The Visitor was a talented player and a well-liked member of the team. He was fast, athletic and had the ability to keep the dugout fun regardless of the score. During one doubleheader, he had a career day: seven hits out of eight trips to the plate. He hit a single, a double, a triple and a home run in one of the games. As a result, the Coach presented him with the game ball that day. This was a tradition that took place after every game. While "game ball" performances didn't occur for every player at every game, at least one time during the season, even the least talented player played well beyond his capability and received the game ball. In fact, the coaching staff enjoyed the game ball tradition every bit as much as the players did.

The Visitor related to Coach during their phone conversation that recently his father celebrated his 60th birthday. At that birthday celebration, the Visitor handed his dad a small gift wrapped box. He told his dad that it was his way of saying "thank you" for all the hard work he had put in over the years to provide for his family. Although Dad couldn't attend many of his son's baseball games, the Visitor told his dad that while he would have loved to have had him there, he fully understood why he couldn't attend and *that he always thought of him at every game. Inside the box was the game ball the Visitor had received on the day of his career double header. The significance of the gift brought tears to the eyes of his dad and put a pretty good sized lump in the throat of the Coach. As a leader, rewards can come in the most inauspicious, yet meaningful ways.*

It is not the purpose of this book to convince anyone to accept a *leadership* position by touting the benefits that make being a leader so rewarding. I will say unabashedly: There are many excellent reasons to stay in the ranks. As a leader, **you** will be held responsible for everything that your team does or fails to do. The tasks your team will need to accomplish will be much too extensive or complicated for you to achieve on your own. The concept of "If you want something done right, do it yourself" doesn't work in a *leadership* position. There simply is no way that you can get it done by yourself. A significant characteristic of an effective and inspirational leader is to involve the team in the process of achieving their objective.

While you may indeed receive a pay raise for accepting a *leadership* role, do yourself a favor. Don't yield to temptation and try to calculate how much you will be making per hour. A leader is a leader 24/7. Making that calculation will show you a disappointing hourly wage. Even when the work day is over and your team invites you to join them for a cold beverage, it is still your responsibility to carry the mantle of *leadership* in word and deed. On occasion and without warning, events will occur to make you and everyone else around you painfully aware that **you** are the leader. You will be expected to react to those events appropriately. How you respond will determine your future as a leader. Sound like fun? It **can** be but you must have the right kind of makeup within. Burning within you must be a willingness to shoulder responsibility in the most taxing of circumstances. I will provide an example, but the pressure it portrays in print doesn't come close the intensity of pressure that can be applied in more significant *leadership* roles. The following example deals with a game, not life and death.

PLAY BALL

Imagine being a baseball player in the seventh game of the World Series. It is the bottom of the ninth inning with one out. There are runners on second and third base and your team is down by one run. The batter ahead of you in the batting order has just stepped into the batter's box. Several possibilities have just surfaced, all of which transpired while you were in the dugout cheering on your teammates, but otherwise did not directly involve you.

Scenario A- The batter gets a base hit. There is good chance two runs will score. Game over. Your team wins. You are not a factor on that play. You and your teammates are World Champions-every baseball player's dream!

Scenario B- The batter receives a base on balls and the runners on second and third base do not score. You come up to bat with the winning runs still on base. The defense will attempt to get you to hit into a play with the potential for you to lose the game. Hit an easy grounder to an infielder and you may start that easy double play for the final two outs. Your team loses and you are the goat. Get a base hit, the winning run scores from second base, and you are the hero.

Scenario C- The batter ahead of you hits into a double play, ending the game. That eliminates any need for you to come to the plate as your team will have lost.

You have no control over any of these situations. Depending upon what the batter ahead of you does, you will be potentially forced into a hero or goat situation. What would you like to have happen? Now consider your answer carefully! It will impact your current aptitude for *leadership*.

The correct answer is **all** the above.

Scenario A- This outcome results in the achievement of your team's goal with no direct involvement on your part in the play and consequently no glory. The right leader is not in it for the glory.

Scenario B- Success or failure has come down to your actions. While it would have been great for the team to win without you providing the hit to make it happen, you should be willing to step into that pressure position when necessary to achieve the team goal.

Scenario C- This is also a correct answer but from a different perspective. If this is your choice, then maybe *leadership* is not yet in your skill set. As a leader, your driving force must be for your team to accomplish its objective even if that sole responsibility is placed squarely on your shoulders.

Personal glory for you should be irrelevant (B). But if it comes down to someone having to be in that decisive position, you must be more than willing for that person to be you. Does that pressure to carry all the responsibility for your team to succeed or fail sound attractive? Does the potential to carry that role increase your heart rate? Does it make you want to jump in and take charge? If so read on! You just may have what it takes to be a leader!

SANTA BARBARA BY THURSDAY

Not long after I retired, drastically reducing my need for neckties, I threw on a t-shirt, helped my 10-year-old Jack Russell Terrier, Powder, into my new Jeep and took off on a 3-week road trip from Denver to the West Coast. Some of my more self-actualized friends like to refer to our trip as a "vision quest." That may have been a bit overdramatic, but in reality, I was sixty years old and starting my second adulthood. I had spent thirty-three years driving a company sedan and I needed some windshield time of my own. My ultimate objective was simple: reconnect with special friends from my past, enjoy some unstructured time to visit the West, and make it home safely.

What happened along the way was partly planned, but the majority was left to fate, divine guidance and dumb luck. We received a lot of all three. I did all the driving of course. Powder, the

Jack Russell, may have been a wonder dog, but apparently, it was her objective to nap through 4,000 miles and five states.

(Before I continue, I fully realize that the relationship of this story to inspirational leadership at first glance is less than obvious, but bear with me. I'm confident that I am going to succeed in pulling all of this together for you.)

We had planned for my wife to meet us two weeks into the road trip in Santa Barbara, California. She would then accompany us back home to Colorado. My intermediate objective was to be in Santa Barbara to meet her by the second Thursday after our departure from Colorado.

Our journey west from Colorado through Utah, Idaho, Oregon, California, Nevada and back home to Colorado was all that I hoped for. The only exception was the lack of time that Powder was awake and enjoying the breathtaking scenery. I've convinced myself that her slumber was her way of saying, "Dad, I have complete confidence in your driving skills, navigational expertise and ability to discover the perfect burger joint for lunch. I'll let you know if I need to "explore the roadside."

At several points, old college buddies who put

us up for the night would inquire about our plans. My answer was always the same: "After Corvallis, Oregon on Sunday night, I just need to be in Santa Barbara by Thursday." My retired friends completely understood. Those still gainfully employed would roll their eyes, make a funny expression and then stare longingly into the distance for a minute or so before returning to the discussion and changing the subject.

Shortly after arriving home my perspective of the trip underwent an interesting transformation. After the successful completion of both my intermediate objective of arriving in Santa Barbara in time to greet my wife (on Thursday of course) and fulfilling my ultimate objective of all of us making it home safely, I began to see a clearer vision of the rewards that our trip provided. Quite a few incredible experiences stand out in my mind. They begin with experiencing, exploring and enjoying Moab, Utah during a stop to visit with my eldest daughter. I avoided the interstate highway system whenever possible and as a result found some of the best mom-and-pop burger spots in this country. I reconnected with old friends from college. I witnessed a breathtaking sunset at Cape Blanco, Oregon while enjoying a fine bottle wine from the

Willamette Valley and a great cigar.

All my objectives for the trip were accomplished. That was our priority as we travelled the back roads of the West. Once I arrived home safely and accomplished my mission, it became apparent that the true reward of the trip lay in the experiences that I enjoyed along the way.

The *leadership* experience is very similar in many ways to my West Coast road trip. Without any doubt, a leader's objective is mission accomplishment linked inseparably to the welfare of the members of the team.

Once the job is done and all your people are accounted for, as the leader you should get to enjoy a cold beverage in retrospective solitude. Before the foam has disappeared or the ice has melted, you will begin to appreciate how enjoyable the journey was. Even those times when you were challenged appear so much better, so much more formative and so much sweeter after the challenge has been conquered. If you unfortunately succumbed to the challenge, if something is learned by all and nobody got hurt, those challenges become a very special experience as well. My blackjack losses in Reno during my road trip fall into that category.

WHAT NOW?

At this point, it is time to revisit the original question. **Why do you want to lead?** This is one of those frequent times in life when you need to be brutally honest with yourself. Don't even consider seeking a *leadership* position unless the only answer in your heart is a version of: "I want to be able to help the people on my team succeed and I know I can do that. I also want to show I care about them, their future and contribute to their success in life." Any response short of that will set you on the road to disappointment, heartache, frustration and failure… all for your teammates! Don't make them suffer because **you** want a better office, a title with the word "manager" in it or a pay raise. However, if your palms begin to sweat and your heart swells with anticipation at the possibility of helping a team or person succeed (quite possibly anonymously to everyone except your team and your leaders), and you can enjoy the value of the challenges along the path - read on. You are starting off with the right attitude. Now let's go find a solid foundation on which to build your *leadership* puzzle!

LEADERSHIP v. MANAGEMENT

"What the hell just happened?" Yesterday, I

was just one of the workers. All that was expected of me was to get my job done right. After quitting time, I had the luxury of leaving my job at work. Nothing to worry about on my time as long as I showed up tomorrow and accomplished what was asked of me. Now the powers that be have decided for some reason, they want to make me a "manager." I even have these snazzy new business cards that say I am the Shift Manager. The problem is, now they are throwing around words like "leadership." Could someone here please make up their minds? Am I a manager or a leader? I would be an idiot to turn down the position, considering the perks that go with it, but it sure would make it easier if I knew what was expected of me."

Sound at all familiar? One of the first challenges newly appointed leaders encounter, once they come to grips with the reality that someone has just anointed them a leader, is the task of identifying the difference between management and **leadership**. Without a healthy dose of **leadership** skills, the management experience will be a difficult and rocky road. Likewise, trying to lead without knowing how to manage can be just as challenging. Unfortunately, the difference between the two is rarely explained or understood. When the difference is made clear, the road ahead becomes much more rewarding and the leader or manager becomes much more effective. Management and *leadership* are not synonymous.

Just because you have the skill set to succeed at one, doesn't mean those skills will transfer to the other. Thankfully, there is a simple differentiation. Imagine the task of painting a room. In the process, all the techniques of taping, cutting in and cleaning up would be useless without the ability to appropriately apply the paint where it belongs. As simple as slopping paint on a wall can be, doing so evenly and with uniform strokes requires a higher level of expertise. Turn me loose on a room and I can guarantee you I can get the can open. I could even assure you that I could get paint on the walls with some of it being where it belonged. Unfortunately, a large portion of it would end up on the wrong surface. Let's imagine that the tasks of preparing the room to be painted are management tasks with appropriately applying the paint where it belongs is *leadership*.

Perspective on the differences between management and *leadership* is gained by applying definitions to both. As a caveat, countless versions of the definition of both management and *leadership* exist. An individual who has experienced significant success in *leadership* positions based on their own style may find some of the definitions contrary to how they have led. So be it. With that in mind, the following are my working definitions of both:

MANAGEMENT:

The appropriate acquisition, maintenance and utilization of resources to support the successful attainment of objectives.

LEADERSHIP:

The ability to get other people to accomplish an objective that **you** want done because **they want** to do it.

It is appropriate at this point to address the concept of "want." As children, we all had a list of things that we "wanted" for our birthdays and holidays. My concept of "want" in *leadership* is significantly different than desiring the newest video game console or a puppy. "Want" may be realizing that a task must be accomplished by someone for the good of the organization. The mission itself may not be desirable. Perhaps the mission is miserable or downright dangerous. At the same time, you and your team know that your organization is the most capable of accomplishing the required goal. Hence if it is to be done, you are the ones who **want** to be assigned the task.

For a leader, being able to get the job done isn't enough. Say your team gets the mission accomplished but right before you turn off the lights, the entire staff steals a key from a keyboard, spits in the coffee maker and bids you "Adios and vaya con dios!" If you are then required to recruit and train a new team before undertaking your next mission, that would reflect a significant shortfall in your *leadership* abilities despite your team's previous mission's success.

Conversely, let's examine the leader of a sales team that exceeds all its sales goals. If at the same time the team has exceeded its budget so severely that the unit's return on investment is minimal, the leader has demonstrated a lack of management abilities.

A simple way to differentiate *leadership* from **management** is to remember that *leadership* is about **people** and **management** is about **things**. The development and publication of standard operating procedures (SOP) is an example of a management requirement. The tasks that relate to *leadership* as it pertains to that SOP are as follows:

1- The leader coaches the team in how to follow the procedures.

2- The leader evaluates the performance of the individual members of the team. The leader must possess the willingness to deliver feedback to correct or deal with shortfalls and to reinforce desired behaviors.

3- The leader sets the example by following those same procedures without fail.

To reinforce, *leadership* is about people and management is about things. Ultimately, to be successful, you will need to master both. There you have it. Now be careful not to kick over that open can of paint!

UNDERSTAND WHAT IS ASKED OF YOU

A little silver-haired woman calls her neighbor and says, "Please come over here and help me. I have a very difficult jigsaw puzzle and I can't figure out how to get started!" Her neighbor asks, "What is it supposed to be when it is finished?" The little woman says, "According to the picture on the box, it is a rooster." Her neighbor decides to go over and help with the puzzle. She lets him in and shows him where she has the puzzle spread all over the table. He studies the pieces for a moment, looks at the box, then turns to her and says, "First of all, no matter what we do, we're not going to be able to assemble these pieces into anything resembling a rooster." He then takes her hand and says, "Secondly, I want you to relax. Let's have a nice cup of tea and then," he says with a deep sigh, "Let's put all the Corn Flakes back in the box."

As the leader of a team, you will be held responsible for everything your team does or fails to do. You might want to look closely at the mission you are being asked to carry out **before** accepting the assignment.

Don't be afraid of what appears to be impossible. Impossible things are happening every day! Need examples? Consider the challenge of putting humans on the surface of the moon. This was a task that was only considered a science fiction fantasy less than a century ago. While the first moon landing captivated the world in 1969, exploring the lunar surface became commonplace when the last Apollo mission was completed in 1972. Have you seen the "Star Wars" series? The masters of special effects have made the impossible seem commonplace. I seriously doubt the phrase "We can't do that!" ever echoes through the halls of Industrial Light and Magic. (Industrial Light and Magic, ILM, is an Academy Award winning motion picture visual effects company conceived and started by George Lucas and now owned by Disney. They brought you the magic of "Star Wars" in 1977.) Multiple computers now populate every room in our homes, and they are immensely more powerful than the first computer that took up the space of an entire room.

The challenge in *leadership* is faced when you are asked to do what seems to be the impossible **without** the resources or support that is required. Ask yourself this key question: "Is successful achievement of goals even possible with the resources we are being given?" No? There is your first *leadership* challenge. Leaders must learn to manage up. The ability to convince those senior to them to obtain the resources they need is an example of that skill. Failing that, the leader must be able to improvise, adapt, or make do with what is at hand. Remember: It's difficult to find the "corner pieces" in a box of Corn Flakes but with some glue and a few colored magic markers, that rooster may soon begin to take shape!

AUTHORITY AND RESPONSIBILITY

In November 2012, one of the most respected men in Major League Baseball resigned as manager of the Colorado Rockies to the considerable disappointment and surprise of players and fans as well as his boss. Jim Tracy was appointed manager of the club May of 2009. He was given the responsibility of turning around a dispirited and underachieving team and returning it to respectability. He succeeded in leading the club to the playoffs that fall. Because of his leadership, he was named the National League Manager of the Year. Shortly after that, he was given a verbal promise by the general manager, (leader) to have a place with the Rockies for as long as he wanted to manage.

In 2012, Tracy encountered a significant conflict between responsibility and authority. The year had begun poorly. Injuries to key starters left their mark and contributed to the team's worst season in history. As they say, "That's baseball!" Injuries are a part of the game that will bite one team hard this season and attack another the next year. Most Rockies fans can comprehend that. If Jim Tracy had remained, there would have been no less enthusiasm by knowledgeable fans on opening day 2013.[1]

Unfortunately, the Rockies leadership team came up with a bad idea in my opinion, which in turn forced Jim Tracy's resignation. Midway through the horrendous losing experience of 2012,

---

[1] www.roxwalkorr.com/2012/20/jim-tracy-contract-extended

the authority to make decisions affecting the future of the club, such as who to promote to the major league club and how many pitches a starting pitcher was to throw before being replaced was taken from Jim. The assistant general manager was given an office in the clubhouse along with the authority to manage the pitchers and to evaluate the coaching staff - both integral parts of the job held by Jim Tracy. This was a blatant affront to the leadership role of Tracy as the manager.

Interestingly, none of the responsibility of turning the team around was removed from Jim's shoulders - just the authority to manage the single most important position on the field, the player that touches the baseball on every play. Although players, fans and executive management all wanted Jim Tracy to return, he resigned after meeting with the assistant general manager following discussions of what the next year held in store. One can only speculate on what transpired during that meeting. Jim Tracy's experience in baseball was extensive enough, including nine years managing at the major league level, for him to have a pretty complete leadership puzzle. The removal of his authority to completely manage the ball club in no way *removed the responsibility that he felt to himself, his players and the fans in helping the team win. Jim was wise enough to realize that without the authority to lead, the responsibility to lead was handicapped. The Rockies committed a cardinal sin with regards to Jim Tracy. They delegated responsibility without delegating the authority that must accompany it.*

Without question, once you assume the mantle of *leadership*, along with it will come the weight of responsibility. As the leader of any team, it is imperative to know that **you** will be held responsible for everything your team does or fails to do. Often, you will be asked to accomplish a task without all the necessary tools you would like. Take heart. This is a great opportunity. There is no need for *leadership* if there are no challenges to be overcome. Ironically, it is victories in those sorts of situations that are the sweetest. Had the 2012 Rockies turned the season around despite the injuries and made the playoffs, one could speculate that Jim Tracy would have considered it his finest year.

There is one thing you want to make sure you have in good supply before accepting a *leadership* position and that is the **authority** to lead. Without the authority to execute your mission as the situation dictates, you may want to pass on the assignment. With any *leadership* opportunity, there will be constraints placed upon you such as budgets, schedules, ethical considerations and logistical support available. Those restrictions make it even more important that you maintain the authority to react to situations as they arise. It has been said that "Every battle plan is excellent-until the first shot is fired." As you approach your objective, whatever it may be, rest assured that you will be shot at in some sense. Ensure that you have the authority and the will to adapt to changing situations as required. That will help you immensely in fulfilling the responsibility you carry on your shoulders.

ASSUMING COMMAND

During a training evolution for several hundred twenty-year-old midshipmen from Naval R.O.T.C. units around the country, one midshipman was given her first experience of assuming command. Allow me to relate her story:

Mid July in Corpus Christi, Texas is no picnic

due to the oppressive heat and humidity. Oh sure, it may be tolerable if you are headed to the beach with a cooler of frosty beverages and a group of friends. However, when you hail from less humid climes and are in a stressful work environment, constantly surrounded by the specter of evaluation, it is difficult to determine if the sweat dripping into your eyes is from the weather, the pressure...or both.

Naval R.O.T.C. midshipmen from various universities around the nation had converged on Corpus Christi Naval Air Station for an aviation evaluation. That was the formal name. Certainly, they would learn about flight, but just as importantly, the Navy would learn about each midshipman's aptitude for leadership as well as their potential for success in flight school in one of the most demanding of environments, that of peer leadership.

Late one morning, a young midshipman was called out from the formation of her classmates. She was informed that she would be assigned the role of Acting Platoon Commander for the next three days. The first order she was to execute was to dismiss her "command" for lunch, gather the platoon in formation afterwards and move the unit on foot to an assigned classroom for a lesson on airfoil principles.

That summer was not one that provided Corpus Christi with any relief from the expected heat and humidity. Periods of instruction alternated between flying actual aircraft (with qualified pilots) to hour upon hour of lectures. Those classroom sessions took place in wooden two-story buildings built during World War II. Air conditioning although present, was an afterthought, provided by two or three small window units working at maximum capacity in each classroom. With 125 fellow students, you were lucky to get one of the 25 coveted seats near one of these units. By staying cool you had a fighting chance to stay awake. That would allow you to avoid the wrath of your active duty instructor by reacting to you dozing off during afternoon classes.

Following lunch, the new Acting Platoon Commander formed up her platoon and marched them two miles from the mess hall to their classroom (not so affectionately known as "The Box"). Upon arriving there were three other platoons already present, standing in formation, awaiting instructions to enter the classroom. Access to the assigned classroom was through a single door at the top of a flight of stairs attached to the outside of the building. Apparently, the other platoon commanders assumed that since they were early for class, they were to wait outside until the door was unlocked and opened. You could say that was a safe assumption, but wrong! Our Acting Platoon Commander figured that if they were going to be waiting in the hot sun, they might as well be doing so on the stairs outside the door to the classroom.

When leading troops in formation, there are certain commands a leader can bark that convert the formation to a single file. Upon hearing those commands from the Acting Platoon Commander, the platoon began ascending the stairs as opposed to standing in formation as the other platoon commanders chose to do. One could not help but hear the murmurs of dissatisfaction arising from the other platoons. When the first *midshipman reached the door, to his surprise, he found it unlocked! The platoon filed into the classroom. Being the first platoon present, they proceeded to dominate the coveted "air conditioner" seats for the rest of the afternoon. Well most of the fortunate platoon did. The Acting Platoon Commander, as is appropriate, was not in one of the "arctic seats" next to the air conditioners for reasons that will become obvious in the Trust chapter. For the rest of the summer assignment, she found it difficult to pay for even a soda whenever a member of her platoon was around.*

The platoon leader in this example did an admirable job demonstrating her initiative and a willingness to take risks. By directing her platoon as she did, she put herself in a position to unfavorably affect her leadership evaluation. Exercising initiative beyond direction as she did can be a risky move. She did so however with her platoon's welfare in mind. At the age of twenty, she found a critical piece to her leadership puzzle.

Shortly after a coalition of military forces from the

free world removed Saddam Hussein and the Iraqi Army from Kuwait in 1991, I had the distinct honor of listening to the commander of that operation, U.S. Army General Norman Schwarzkopf, speak about leadership. Here was a man that attained the rank of General in the U.S. Army. His final career victory was to defeat the fourth largest army in the world in the space of one hundred hours. "Defeat" is probably an inappropriate term. "Rout" is more like it. Imagine how complete his *leadership* puzzle must have been after such a career! As I sat in the audience, I was thrilled at the prospect of collecting an overwhelming number of puzzle pieces from this master of command. My only concern was that my notebook didn't contain enough sheets of paper to capture all that I was about to hear. To my surprise, I received just two... but they were two of the most profound I have ever heard!

General Schwarzkopf helped me realize that as much as there is to learn about *leadership*, those that are most successful have an ability to cut through the fog and focus on what is most important. One of the points that the general shared with us was Rule 13, which directly applies to this early stage of any leader's development. The other, Rule 14, will apply to everything you do as a leader:

Rule 13: When placed in command, take charge!

Rule 14: Do the right thing!

While Rules 1 through 12 certainly do exist, and are well worth reviewing, Rules 13 and 14 have the greatest impact at this point in this conversation. Quite honestly, the simplicity and completeness of Rules 13 and 14 are comprehensive enough to be all one needs to know about beginning the *leadership* process. I will expand on Rule 14 by providing some examples of what defines the "**right thing**" as we progress through the various *leadership* skills that help to form the image for the *leadership* puzzle, we will explore it in depth in "The *Leadership* Spotlight." As far as Rule 13 is concerned, it is a significantly critical rule to include in our discussion of "The Foundations of *Leadership*."

RULE 13: WHEN PLACED IN COMMAND, TAKE CHARGE

Every leader will have their Day One. Few leaders

will sleep the night prior to that Day One. When it is your turn you may be just a bit unsure of yourself and wonder whether you are ready. In fact, a little self-doubt is probably a good thing. It is now that you will glimpse one of the four corner puzzle pieces (from a very different perspective).

It is important to **trust** that the person who has appointed you to lead your new team knows what they are doing in choosing you for your assignment. You may be unsure that you know all there is to know about successful **leadership**. Rest assured that you don't, but that is okay. It is vital you **trust** that the leader who has chosen you for this position is confident that, while you don't know everything yet, you know enough to begin the journey. Get a mighty grip on that confidence. When you step out in front of your team for the first time, hold your head up, look directly at them and speak with authority. Know what you want to say and say it with conviction! Referees and umpires in all sports learn this on their Day One. While controlling the play of a baseball game, there will be numerous calls that are questionable even from the umpire's perspective. No matter! Whether the umpire is certain of the call in his mind or not, he must **sell it**! A weak call will put everyone in doubt and result in profanity, spit, flying dust and thrown bases, before or after the inevitable ejection. There is a saying: "Never let them see you sweat!" As a new leader take that advice to heart.

Be confident in the knowledge that most of the members of your team want you to be a good leader. They are willing to give you the benefit of the doubt, but their judgment will be swift. Make sure you are prepared. Take command enthusiastically and confidently. You will alienate no one that you will need to count on, if you do it with a simple philosophy.

Regardless of their experience, no veteran leader knows all about their new organization on Day One. Consequently, you will rarely see an effective or accomplished leader try to change the entire organization immediately. This is true regardless of whether their predecessor was fired or promoted. Promise yourself that you will take the time to observe how the team works. Ask questions. Gather data. Focus on mission accomplishment and on the welfare of your team concurrently. If you observe policies and procedures and have doubt as to their relevance to mission accomplishment or personnel welfare, discuss them with your junior leaders as well as with your boss. It is quite likely that those policies or procedures are in place for reasons of which you are unaware. You will have plenty of time to make necessary changes to improve the functioning of your team. Don't try to do it all on the first day or accomplish it based on your solitary observations. If you can make a good case for making change, and have obtained buy in, you will generate significantly greater support from your team than by simply stating: "Because **that** is the way I want it done!" If you can't come up with a better reason than that for the change, don't make it!

Similarly, once you make the decision to accept a *leadership* role, very few things can be more damaging to your first impression as excessive hesitancy. A violation of Rule 13 (When placed in command, take charge) will be observed immediately by those to whom you report as well as those that report to you.

During my tenure in corporate life, I watched a newly appointed sales manager make this very mistake, and he never recovered. Prior to his appointment to the position that he had expressed a desire to fill, he was posted to another city in a leadership training position. After a year or two training to become a sales manager, his selection to lead his own team was announced. As you may imagine, the word spread rapidly through the grapevine to his waiting colleagues. Initially there was quite a bit of concern because word had also spread that this location was not his first choice. It was a full six weeks before he made his first visit to meet his new team in the team's headquarters city. His hesitancy to take charge of his district actually reflected a lack of desire, commitment and interest in his new team, its location and mission. Ironically his error turned out to be a red flag signaling a general lack of leadership skills altogether.

As debilitating as hesitancy can be to a newly appointed leader, overzealousness can prove to be just as damaging. It is extremely rare to find an individual who is completely enamored with the concept of change. The corporate world has invested significant resources trying to convince and cajole people to embrace change with a smile and a hopeful vision of the future. The reason these resources must be invested to accomplish that attitude shift is because change has the potential to be uncomfortable for anyone. No matter how certain an individual is that "With all this horse manure in the box, there must be a pony in here somewhere," there will always be a bit of apprehension with any change in *leadership*.

As a new leader, it is normal for you to want to make your mark and make sure everyone knows who the boss is. Relax. Unless **your** boss has given you specific marching orders to immediately take some form of specific action, allow yourself a period of time to observe how things are done on your new team. During your initial meeting with your teammates, simply introduce yourself, confirm your *commitment* to the unit's overall mission, and provide assurance to your new charges that you are going to make decisions regarding any changes based upon **your** observations, and not those of your predecessor. Your position will be anchored as you respect your team for what they have already accomplished.

The concept of a "clean slate" will go a long way in allowing your good performers to rest easy with a change of *leadership* and perform to their abilities. Those who have been performing below par will be faced with the decision to either raise their bar or to suffer the wrath of their new leader. Those in the middle of the pack may see an opportunity to raise their game and to become one of the stars.

In summary, don't be afraid to take command of your team. They expect it. At the same time, as you are taking command, be certain your actions are related to doing the **right thing** for your team. Does that sound challenging? You bet! Nowhere in this book will you find a promise that *leadership* is easy. That's why the rewards are so significant and why effective inspirational *leadership* is so rare in the experience of most of us. If it was easy, everyone would do it!

WOMEN IN *LEADERSHIP*

The number of women who hold *leadership* positions in Fortune 500 companies is dismally low. Since 2009 when the percentage was 13.5 percent, it inched its way upward to only 16.3 percent in 2015-16.

My purpose is not to discuss the whys and why nots of those statistics. The topics and fundamentals addressed in this book have equal significance to women as well as to men. It is important however to draw attention to the challenges and opportunities that women face as leaders. As a result, each section of this book will address how the topics addressed in general apply specifically to women in *leadership* positions.

For all of us, men or women, as we enter our first *leadership* role there is a natural tendency to seek guidance as to what to do first. I would describe that search as "looking over your shoulder" to reflect on how you were led in the past, and attempt to learn from those experiences. Personally, that strategy worked out well for me, but I am a man. I was fortunate to have had competent leaders, both male and female, whose behaviors, if followed, would stand me in good stead. For a woman, even with her previous leaders also being competent, chances are a large majority of them were men. That is not a disadvantage, but it is a limitation. As a result, without specific considerations or observations of the special skills that women can bring to the *leadership* position, as well as the unique challenges they face because of their gender, one would expect those women to learn primarily from the behaviors demonstrated by previous leaders who were men. I am not disparaging the *leadership* skills females can learn from competent male leaders. However, it places women at a disadvantage if they have not also been able to witness the different and unique *leadership* strengths that leaders of their own gender have brought to the field.

ENOUGH WINDUP! THROW THE BALL!

With that, let's wrap up this discussion on "The Foundations of *Leadership*." It's time to open the box and seek out the critical corner pieces to get you started on your puzzle. Hearty congratulations on accepting the challenge and accepting it for the right reasons. You have already proven yourself to be in the top echelon of the population as far as your ability to make this a better world, one *leadership* challenge at a time!

COMMITMENT

"There is a difference between interest and commitment. When you're interested in doing something, you do it only when it's convenient. When you're committed to something, you accept no excuses-only results!"

--Kenneth H. Blanchard

63

RICHARD BROWN

COMMITMENT

While the official mascot of the high school may have been the "Thunderbirds", anyone familiar with the day to day activities may have correctly said it was "Apathy." The school colors highlighting the walls of the hallways may have been green and gold, but the colors of the gang that you were trying to avoid were more important. The 2,000 students, 88 percent being minority in a school with mostly Caucasian teachers, lived mostly in poverty in the surrounding neighborhoods. Their mere presence at school could be considered a moral victory. For most the kids, school simply served to keep the local cops out of their hair as they conducted whatever less than legal business they needed to conduct. Gaining an education was the last reason most of them were even in school.

The students, loitering in those hallways well after the bell rang signifying class had begun, hardly noticed the "old white dude." It mattered little that they didn't recognize him. Why would they? He had just been hired as assistant principal. I will refer to him simply as AP. His presence was completely irrelevant to whatever the students were doing instead of being in class.

AP promised himself that day that he would not settle for any moral victories. He resolved not to manage from inside an office, but to lead from the front. Instead of accepting the assignment as a stepping stone to one of the schools in a more upscale community, he began an effort amongst the faculty to modify the culture. He believed they could create opportunities for kids to succeed and go on to college. The commitment he demanded from his student body was simple: "If you want to come here, you're going to be a student." Gang colors were prohibited and an innovative system of discipline was instituted that involved students in a restorative versus a punitive manner.

Before the freshman who noticed AP in the halls on that first day even began to prepare for graduation four years later, something incredible happened. A local police official with the department's gang unit noted that in his dealings with teens (even former gang members), they began to speak highly of the school. "They have told me they prefer to go to that school because they feel safe there, that they're listened to, and that the school does the best it can to provide a safe learning environment for them."

Within four years of AP's arrival, the school ranked third among high schools in the state in terms of students earning advance college credit. Four hundred and nine students in all had accumulated more than three thousand college credit hours while still attending high school. As an important sidelight, this school also had a principal who not only hired AP and let him run the program, but focused all the attention for the school's success on AP. That is real leadership. As Harry Truman said, "It is amazing what you can accomplish if you do not care who gets the credit!"[2]

A basic understanding of the foundations of *leadership* should begin to shed some light on the most elementary requirements for effective and inspirational *leadership*. The acceptance of a position of *leadership* responsibility requires a willingness to go beyond involvement. Following closely is the all or nothing acceptance to commit to both the accomplishment of the objective, as well as to the

---

[2] http://www.denverpost.com/news/ci_22752425?stop Redirect=true   Denver Post , Kevin Simpson

welfare of those who stand beside you and help you accomplish that objective.

Unfortunately, this concept of *commitment* may be one of the most misunderstood in today's world. Many consider *commitment* to be synonymous with the term **involvement**. While the two may be related, it is critical to understand the difference when you are dealing with the welfare of those individuals on your team, as well as the mission to which you have been entrusted. Let me demonstrate an example of how America's colleges have contributed to this misunderstanding among a segment of the population that produces a high percentage of our nation's future leaders.

Keep an eye on the sports pages of your local newspaper. Every community has a high school superstar. Football season happens to be when they get the most press, so let us examine what occurs in the fall each year. Throughout the autumn, you will hear about the next great player destined to be highly recruited by major colleges across the country. On occasion, during a slow sports news week, they may even appear on the cover of our country's major sports magazines. Should the superstar decide to attend a particular college, the sports reporters will tell you that Joe Superstar has "committed" to attend the college of his choice. The terms used are not "interested in attending Football U." Neither will you hear that he has "University of Northern Football at the top of his list." It is usually stated that Joe Superstar has "committed to attend Football Polytechnic University in the fall."

Now wait until the first week of February of the following year. That is National Letter of Intent Signing period. Anything said up until this day by the press regarding a *commitment* from an athlete couldn't be further from the truth. Frequently, you will see many players sign with a college other than the one they had previously committed to. No actual *commitment* on the part of a player takes place until a letter of intent is signed. Until then the athlete's desire is better referred to in any of 100 other more appropriate terms such as interest, excitement, etc. No wonder there is such a misuse and misunderstanding of the concept of *commitment*. Our society instills the wrong definition into the minds of seventeen and eighteen-year-old future leaders and then pastes it all over the newspaper! The problem is not the fault of the athlete, but the improper definition of *commitment* as defined by sports reporters, athletic directors and head coaches.

COMMITMENT v. INVOLVEMENT

It is not uncommon for clarity to come in the

simplest of forms. I have searched for more than a decade for an academic, highbrow analogy to clearly differentiate between involvement and commitment. Alas, the simplest of explanations that I was given as a young leader cannot be surpassed. ***Commitment*** and involvement can best be explained when contemplating a bacon and egg breakfast. In the participation of preparing this cholesterol laden plate full of heaven, the chicken was certainly involved, but it was the pig that demonstrated true commitment.

As always, when definitions are confused, it is best to start from the beginning and establish the one definition that you are going to work with. I can best define both ***commitment*** and involvement as follows:

INVOLVEMENT:

A desire to accomplish a mission, depending upon the obstacles encountered.

For example:

What is said- "Sure Bob. I can give you a ride to the airport Saturday at 6:00 am."

What is thought- "Saturday morning at 6:00 am? Yeesh! There is that party I am going to on Friday night. I would hate to miss it! I should be able to provide the ride for Bob, barring any unforeseen developments such as a killer hangover or forgetting to set the alarm. Ah…that's not going to happen."

COMMITMENT:

A determination to accomplish a mission despite the obstacles involved.

For example:

What is said- "Sure Bob. I can give you a ride to the airport Saturday at 6:00 am."

What is thought- "Saturday morning at 6:00 am? Yeesh! There is that party I was invited to on Friday night. I would hate to miss it. I should be able to provide the ride for Bob, barring any unforeseen developments, such as a killer hangover, forgetting to set the alarm, etc. Ah…that's not going to happen. [Enter *commitment*]. I could forgo drinking alcohol. That would avoid the hangover. I could set multiple alarms and have Bob call me at a certain time to ensure I am awake. Bob is a good friend and he's done a lot for me in the past. This flight is critical to him and he needs my help. There will be other parties. I'll just pass on this one and get a good night's rest."

Commitment is a determination to get the mission

accomplished despite the difficulty presented by obstacles that may arise. Inherent in the acceptance of a *leadership* role is your willingness to demonstrate *commitment* as opposed to just being involved. Successful teams are always led by committed individuals. Champion organizations are not only led by committed leaders, but have a front line that demonstrates a high level of *commitment* as well.

WHAT THEY EXPECT OF YOU

As a leader, you have been singled out by those senior to you because they believe you can bring something special to their organization. This fact is not to be taken lightly! Perhaps you were a rank and file member of the team prior to your appointment. If your performance in that role was exceptional, you may have caught the attention of someone who thought you had the potential to lead. Possibly you are new to the organization and your experience and behaviors have shown something that reflects dedication and skill. Congratulations! Colleagues of yours have "rolled the dice" and asked you to help them achieve their goals and dreams. Often, they have invested significant time and effort in the organization. Obviously, they determined that they need assistance in the way of mission accomplishment, and they chose to **you** from among several others also qualified to be part of that effort. That deserves your commitment to them in return.

In your *leadership* role, you will bear a heavy responsibility to your leaders as well as to those you lead. They both will be expecting your *commitment.* While motivation varies with members of organizations, rarely does it begin at a low level. Usually, people accept jobs and join teams with the best of intentions. Your role as their leader will do much to determine if this effort will better their lives or not.

Let us explore the work environment. The enjoyment that most people get out of the eight to ten hours per day they spend at work usually has little to do with all the actual tasks that the work requires. If the daily tasks were unpleasant to them, they probably wouldn't (or shouldn't) have taken the job in the first place. The determining factor as to whether they are happy in their job often is their relationship with their boss. As we will discuss, there are many factors that may influence this relationship, but foremost is the knowledge by the employee that their leader is committed to helping them succeed. If you take care of your people and are committed to the mission, your team will take care of you. A discussion on *leadership* could just about stop right there, but it won't. We still have three puzzle pieces to find!

Simply put, *leadership* is an honor that requires *commitment* from you to both those you serve as well to those that have chosen you for the task. That is NOT a typo. If you are willing to accept the concept that you work **for** your team as opposed to them working **for you**, while you report to those senior to you, you have taken a huge step in becoming an effective and inspirational leader!

If you are not quite ready to provide *commitment*, then do yourself, your seniors and those who you will lead a favor and turn down the honor of *leadership*. It is no reflection on you as a person if you choose not to be a leader. Maybe it's not your dream. Maybe your life circumstances prevent you from providing the *commitment* required now. There is no shame in that. Be honest with yourself as well as those who would like you to lead. Take a pass on shouldering the huge *commitment* that will be expected of you as a leader, if *leadership* is not something that motivates you for the right reasons.

STAIR STEPS OF *COMMITMENT*

So, the call just came in and you have accepted the sought-after *leadership* position. Take some time to celebrate the hard work that got you to this exalted and rewarding role. Having fun? Get over it! As a rank and file member, what was considered exceptional will now be the minimally acceptable behavior for you as a leader. Satchel Paige, a baseball legend, once said "Don't look back, something may be gaining on you!" As a leader, nothing could be more accurate. Never forget, that should your *commitment* level as a leader fall to a point where mission accomplishment or personnel welfare is at stake, you stand a great possibility of being replaced. Those senior to you owe that to those who have been placed in your charge. There is always some ambitious, fresh-faced individual who would love to have your position. At successively higher levels of *leadership*, the expected *commitment* from the leader will increase. As a leader, it is critical that you understand and accept that reality.

A student in a classroom is expected to complete assignments as required. Some students will make an additional *commitment* to not only complete the assigned work, but will also do extra credit assignments. Frequently those students become leaders in the classroom. A teacher however is expected to demonstrate an increased level of *commitment* above even those students who excel. The creation of lesson plans, grading papers at home on weekends and coming into class early to help those students who are struggling are all levels of *commitment* expected of those in positions of educational *leadership*.

A player on a sports team is expected to be at practice and games on time and to put out maximum effort. Leaders on the same team will frequently make the choice to arrive early and stay late to put in extra work to improve their skills. Team captains are expected to demonstrate additional effort in the dugout and on the field. The coach will be expected to demonstrate everything he asks of the captains and beyond. It is the coach's role to arrive before the team is present and stay until the last player has departed. In addition, planning game strategy, evaluating each player's performance trends, and taking time to provide further instruction to those that may be struggling are all the responsibility of the coach and no one else. In addition, the task of identifying and recognizing those that may be in the middle of the pack, yet are demonstrating improvement are duties that any coach worth his or her salt will relish.

TO WHERE ARE YOU LEADING US?

The act of demonstrating *commitment* to those we lead can come in many ways. A valid question to ask is "*Commitment* to what?" No group needs a leader if there is nothing to accomplish. As the leader, you will have a say in what those goals will be. First and foremost, the mission of your parent organization is paramount. It should always supersede any goals that you identify for your team. At the same time, different teams at different levels of development are expected to contribute to the main goal, but **what** they contribute may differ from team to team. This is a clear example of where *leadership* becomes a factor.

One of the earliest expectations of you as a leader is to determine where you want your team to go. Utilizing a teacher and a coach as examples, perhaps your mission is to have your students master a certain set of learning objectives during this semester. Winning the state championship is certainly an accomplishment many coaches would love to achieve. While it is important to strive to attain goals that are challenging, it is just as important to be realistic about the abilities of your team. Perhaps with a team of underclassmen who are rebuilding from losing several starting seniors from last year's squad, achieving a 50/50 win loss record is a stretch. For a teacher in an underserved school located in an area stricken with poverty, the goal of merely increasing attendance over last semester may be sufficient. This is where learning about your team as discussed in "The Foundations of *Leadership*" comes into play. You may not be able to identify a goal for your team on Day One. That's okay if setting an appropriate goal remains your top priority.

As you learn the strengths and weaknesses of your

organization, take a step back and identify what you want your team to look like at the end of a given period. This is the concept of "Begin with the End in Mind" as presented by Steven Covey in "The Seven Habits of Highly Successful People." It should provide the genesis of your mission statement, which is a required element for any team. What do **you** want this group to look like at the end of the semester or year? Once you identify what that looks like you can begin to plan a strategy to achieve that goal. If you have identified a specific goal that is attainable but still requires your team to stretch their reach, you can begin to plan to implement the tactics that will get you there…or beyond!

COMMUNICATION

A mission statement is one of those things that is written about ad infinitum in business journals. Mission statements fill a critical role in virtually every organization. I dare say that the absence of a mission statement should be grounds for the dismissal of any leader that has been in their post for any significant period of time. Unfortunately, in many organizations, mission statements have a lot less going for them than the weather. A saying that many people attribute to Mark Twain (albeit even that citing is controversial) is "Everybody talks about the weather, but nobody does anything about it!" Whether it was Mr. Twain or someone else, here is a paraphrasing that you can contribute to me without question: "Mission statements in subpar organizations are not like the weather: **Nobody** talks about them, much less does anything about them." In some organizations, they serve a similar function as a Halloween decoration. They come out once a year to be published in the annual report, and then get put away the next day.

A well-written, realistic, attainable and specific mission statement does absolutely **nothing** for an organization unless it is published and effectively communicated so that it is the guiding principle regarding the behavior of every member of the organization. Imagine hiring a group of new employees, but never informing them of their job description. In the same vein, imagine taking a group on a hike into the wilderness with no identified route or destination. The implications are disastrous.

MAINTAIN RELEVANCE OF PURPOSE

Ideally a well-written, thoroughly published and internalized mission statement should serve the purpose of guiding every behavior within an organization. If there is a desire to deviate from its guiding direction, one of two things should be done. Either the behavior should be altered to bring it in line with the mission statement, or the mission statement itself should be updated. Periodically, the mission statement should be reviewed for pertinence and to ensure that the guiding principles are coherent with the actual goals of the organization. A mission statement is important, but it is not a religious document intended to be followed at all costs.

During the formative years of Professional Resource Enhancement, we worked closely with a very successful youth sports organization. Its mission statement emphasized the importance of developing successful individuals through sports. Nowhere in their purpose did they emphasize the development of champions in the various activities that they sponsored. It is a reality in this particular environment that having national and Olympic champions with origins in your organization is a pretty important claim to fame, and in fact, this club had produced over one hundred Olympic athletes. Ignoring that dimension of their purpose in their mission statement had generated significant conflict amongst the powers behind the club. What was their solution? They modified the mission statement to include a phrase that mentioned a goal of developing champions. This resulted in three benefits:

1- There was no more grousing from the board,

donors and alumni about not focusing on the development of champions.

2- Recognition of the history of the club and its contribution to the success of athletes from many nations, not just the USA became a reality.

3- Continued emphasis of the importance of developing successful individuals. An Olympic berth did not **define** success for a member of the club, but neither was it less than relevant.

COMMITMENT TO MISSION; *COMMITMENT* TO PEOPLE

Regardless of their specific occupations, veterans and members of our nation's armed forces display the ultimate in *commitment* when they take their oath of office. It is said that they are someone who:

"At one point in their lives, wrote a blank check made payable to the United States of America for an amount of up to and including their life."

--Gene Castignetti
Directory of the National Memorial Cemetery of the Pacific

In Appendices A and B of this publication are

reprints of the text of official citations of two veterans who displayed the ultimate in *commitment*. They are not examples of *leadership*, but they do exemplify *commitment*. One's *commitment* was to the mission he was assigned and the other's *commitment* was to those with whom he served. It is possible for any leader to face a very difficult dilemma, and that is the case for the Marine documented in Appendix B. His actions were in opposition to an order to **not** attempt to assist his comrades. If you are committed to your mission, as well as to the welfare of your people, the possibility of a conflict between the two can be very real. I will not pretend to provide you with a formula for choosing which to follow. Should you find yourself in such a dilemma, the more puzzle pieces you have successfully joined together, the easier your decision will be. Perhaps this sentiment will help: Your mission **always** comes first, but your people **never** come second.

WOMEN IN *LEADERSHIP* : *COMMITMENT*

Numerous romantic comedies have been released from Hollywood that find an appropriate foil in portraying a young man in his late twenties who is afraid of the concept of *commitment* to a romantic relationship. While that example may work in the world of young love, it is a bit different in the field of *leadership*.

There is nothing present or absent in the genetic makeup of a member of either gender that should result in any problem for them to demonstrate *commitment* when it is required. The only challenge that some of us struggle with because of demonstrating *commitment* is the application of a label. Put a veteran leader in front of a room of a newly formed team of hires, recruits, students or athletes and that experienced leader will have no problem making it very clear what the leader and the organization, will expect of them. At the end of the "in no uncertain terms" orientation, it is quite possible (in fact likely) that some of the less motivated in the room will slap a label on the leader as a "hard ass." Possibly something like the phrase "mean mutha" might even be thrown about. If somebody falls short of what is expected of them, they should hear about it. If that deficiency happens to risk the accomplishment of the mission or the welfare of the rest of the team, there is a problem and it will need to be addressed. Those labels that get thrown around under the breath of some in the audience can tend to have an interesting effect on new leaders.

As the result of a misplaced priority to be liked as opposed to respected and obeyed, labels can be a stumbling block. For some women in that situation there is a trip wire that, when activated, can change the game significantly for her as a leader. It is a label that starts with the letter "B." I will let you take it from there. For men, it is difficult to identify the one specific word that will stimulate a similar reaction, but the concept is still germane. Regardless of gender, it is a mistake to let an overheard disparaging comment generate a damaging self evaluation. I don't mean to imply at all that such reaction is inappropriate or immature, it is just reality. I will say that the best thing a leader can do is accept the fact that you **will** hear those various labels. The best thing you can do is to redefine them.

"Nervousness" and "excitement" provoke very similar physiological responses in the human body. The primary difference is the label that we apply to those emotions. When you feel the butterflies in your gut, the sweat on your palms, the increased heart rate and breathing, it is either nervousness or excitement. Accept the fact that it is a physiological response called "Flight or Fight" preparing you to confront an obstacle. Label that response excitement and you have taken the first step to conquering the obstacle.

Whenever you hear the "B" word as a woman, or whatever term similarly affects you as a man, know that you have gotten their attention. They are beginning to get the idea of your awesome level of *commitment* to both your organization's goals, as well as to their individual welfare. Conduct some independent research on the late Prime Minister Margaret Thatcher. Her nickname was "The Iron Lady" which she wore with a badge of honor, yet always remained first and foremost, a lady.

COMMITMENT: THE FIRST STEP

In the event you read this book in its entirety, you will come close to being able to recite this section by heart. That is because it will appear more than once as the conclusion to a chapter. This was done so that if only one chapter is deemed pertinent to be read at any one time, this critical message would not be missed..

I describe the *leadership* relationship as being similar to any personal relationship. The three primary qualities of a leader, *trust, caring,* and *commitment* are vital to any relationship. They are critical in a romantic relationship, a family relationship, a sales relationship, and a platonic relationship. When all three are present, the relationship is at its peak. Remove one element, and the relationship can still function, just not at as high of a level. Remove two elements and the relationship is at serious risk of failing.

The *leadership* relationship is unique in that it

requires a leader. In all cases regarding the three qualities I identified, it is up to the leader to **take the first step**. As their leader, you have the benefit of information your teammates do not have. When you bring on new team members, **you** have the responsibility of ensuring they know what is expected of them. That may mean covering it more than once or in more than one fashion. Communication is a command responsibility. It is simply not acceptable for any of your teammates to ever say with sincerity, "I had no idea that was expected of me." It's understood that people can use that excuse to shirk responsibility, but if a lack of communication is truly what caused the shortfall, the responsibility falls **directly** upon the leader. As a leader, it is up to you to accept the *commitment* to let your team know what you expect of them.

TRUST

"The best executive is the one who has sense enough to pick good people to do what he wants done, and self-restraint enough to keep from meddling with them while they do it."

--Theodore Roosevelt

"To drop dead is honorable in the line of duty, whereas to quit is the highest form of dishonor."

--Colonel John W. Ripley, U.S.M.C

RICHARD BROWN

TRUST

It was Major Bruce Crandall, a helicopter pilot, who Lieutenant Colonel Hal Moore depended on to get soldiers to LZ X-Ray in Vietnam's Ia Drang Valley. This battle in November 1965 would turn out to be the most horrific battle to date in the Vietnam War. But Crandall didn't just get people in – he got them out, too.

The landing zone was the scene of a fierce attack by the enemy, and the remaining helicopters bringing in soldiers were told to turn around and return to base. When Crandall got there, he discovered that medevac help going in had also been stopped. Medical evacuation was not his mission, but he wasn't about to leave those wounded men behind. He also knew that the soldiers still fighting were about to run out of ammunition. So, without asking anyone, he quickly recruited his buddy, Major Ed Freeman. They began to fly back and forth to the battle in unarmed and extremely vulnerable helicopters.

Hours later, he had flown 22 times into what

soldiers later called the "Valley of Death." He flew three different helicopters during 14 hours because two were so damaged they couldn't stay in the air. Crandall and his volunteers rescued 70 of the 78 wounded men, as well as providing ammunition and much needed water.

Crandall served a second tour in Vietnam and retired as a Colonel but his extraordinary actions that day in November 1965 weren't forgotten. He and his buddy Major Ed Freeman were both awarded the Medal of Honor, our nation's highest award, although Crandall's didn't come until 2007. He'll always be a hero to the soldiers who fought in the Ia Drang Valley. One said, "Major Crandall's actions were without questions the most valorous I've observed of any helicopter pilot in Vietnam," and another said, "I will always be in awe of Major Bruce Crandall." Crandall merely said, "They were my people down there, and they trusted in me to come and get them."³

When soldiers, or any type of teammates, **know** the *commitment* shared for and from each other and can *trust* that it is a true *commitment*, their performance

---

³ NATIONAL INFANTRY MUSEUM & SOLDIER CENTER: http://www.nationalinfantrymuseum.org/31days-31stories/

potential is unparalleled. These are the teams that routinely defeat superior odds in accomplishing their mission. It matters little whether that mission is related to in combat, education, athletics or business.

To address any of the fundamentals of **leadership** from a military perspective, particularly with respect to combat, presents its own inherent set of challenges. (**Trust** me! I've gotten heat for this before in the business environment, but the whole Marine thing keeps me forging on!) According to the 2010 Census, less than one percent of the country's population currently serves in the military. Only seven percent of the American population alive in 2010 could identify themselves as veterans of the armed services. That number equates to only twenty-three million of us. To complicate the issue, to address women in **leadership** from a military or veteran's perspective, it is important to remember that only eight percent of the veteran population is female.

With those figures in mind, the odds that you are currently serving in the military are miniscule. Even the odds that you are a veteran of any conflict since World War II are extreme small. While that certainly presents me with a challenge, it also presents an opportunity for all of us. **Leadership** is an integral part of military training at all levels. Unlike most positions in industry, the frank survival of people is dependent on the quality of the leaders in the chain of command. In corporate life, an egotistical boss may generate unfavorable turnover or poor morale. A hesitant, uncommitted, untrustworthy and uncaring manager may have similar results. In the face of combat, those same *leadership* deficiencies may result in bloodshed, death, or the defeat of our country as a nation. The stakes in the military and in civilian life of ineffective *leadership* can be incredibly high. That fact should be what draws corporate, educational and athletic America to learn from the lessons that our active duty military can teach us. It is shortsighted to dismiss them as unique to our fighting forces. *Trust* is foremost among those lessons.

While "great" may be too strong an adjective to describe the discussions that take place as to what motivates troops to perform in combat, it is still a topic of considerable academic study. National interests, American ideals and freedom certainly are factors. It would be difficult to find a combat veteran who disagrees that *trusting* the *commitment* of the guy fighting next to you to "watch your back" is a primary motivation that results in victories on the battlefield against superior odds. It also can explain the motivation behind incredible acts of valor and courage.

Appendices A and B relate two instances of

commitment towards what is considered beyond the call of duty. One describes the *commitment* to mission of Captain John W. Ripley, USMC in Vietnam. The other account describes the *commitment* to his comrades in arms of Corporal Dakota Meyer, USMC. While their exploits took place decades and half a world apart, *commitment* is the common thread. You will see that they both incorporate the powerful fundamental of *trust* as well. Your buddy's mere presence on the battlefield reflects his *commitment*. The fact that you **know** your buddy will carry out his orders, even to include "die in place" next to you, and *trust* that none of them will abandon you, or leave you on the battlefield, even if it means disobeying a direct order or sacrificing their own life, is a powerful motivator. I encourage you to read both accounts now. Imagine the success that we would see in business, education and coaching activities if *commitment* and *trust*, as demonstrated by these individuals, could be counted on in those endeavors of *leadership*.

While in your role as a leader, no matter if it is as a sales manager, coach, teacher or fraternity president, I fervently hope that you never need to save the life of one of your charges by helping them avoid a gunman. Nevertheless, the tragic experiences at Columbine, Virginia Tech, Newtown, San Bernardino, and

Orlando, among too many others, where innocents were faced with deadly gunfire paint that extreme situation as certainly possible. Altering the life of a student or employee by helping them succeed can parallel the contribution you make by helping them to escape a shooter or rendering emergency first aid. In these instances, you will have the opportunity to provide a multitude of influences that will affect their lives as profoundly as if you had stopped their bleeding or removed them from harm's way.

BE CONFIDENT

As discussed in the fundamentals of *leadership*, as a newly appointed leader your first opportunity to display the *trust* that you have in those who chose you to lead is to observe Rule 13: When placed in command, take charge. I realize that I am repeating myself, but know you have proven that you have what it takes to assume your *leadership* role, and with sufficient humility and *commitment*, develop into the leader that your people deserve…even if you are not there yet.

NEVER ASK, BUT SEEK

Whatever your *leadership* assignment is, you will either have come up through the ranks with a significant degree of familiarity for the duties and work conditions of those you lead, or you will be hired from outside the organization. It matters little in which situation you find yourself. You can still be an effective coach even if you have never played all the positions on the team, or even played any at the level that you are coaching. Experience may be the best teacher, but it is not the only member of the faculty. Teachers, coaches, and second lieutenants have all stepped out in front of their teams on their own Day One with no actual hands on experience for every job requirement of those they would lead. Surviving that moment in the spotlight depends on two critically important corollaries of **leadership**. (These don't get to be official "puzzle pieces", but don't let that diminish their importance.) The new leader disregards them at their peril:

1. **Never ask someone to do something that you have not done or would not do yourself.**

Before you institute new policies, establish standards or provide direction, examine what you are asking of your team. The potential exists that it is a task you have never personally undertaken yourself. As a result, you may have little perspective on how that task affects the person who needs to accomplish it. Solution: roll up your sleeves and lend a hand. Ask the expert you are working with to show you their job.

There is no need for you to spend your entire career as one of those in the trenches. You have the potential as a leader to help your team accomplish their goal in more significant ways. Demonstrate you have a working knowledge through either experience, or willingness to try what you are asking your people to do. Then it will be easier for your team to know that they can *trust* you to be able to relate to the duties you will assign them.

2. Seek input from your team leaders who have done the job themselves on a long-term basis.

No one expects you to be an expert on **every** detail of the tasks that are accomplished by your teammates daily. What they want to know is that they can *trust* you to be familiar with their duties and that you respect their expertise in their specialties. Your job is one of *leadership*, and that is not a technical job. Hire good people to get the work done. Make them aware of what you expect of them and then get out of their way. Periodic follow up is necessary to ensure that you can *trust* them to perform as you have directed, but remember what Will Rogers said:

"There are three kinds of men:
The ones that learn by reading.
The few who learn by observation.
The rest of them have to pee on the electric fence

and find out for themselves."

SET THE EXAMPLE

As with all three of the fundamentals of *leadership*, you will have numerous opportunities to demonstrate that you *trust* those who are on your team to assist you in accomplishing whatever mission with which your organization is tasked. Early on in your *leadership* experience you will have your first opportunity to bask in the light of "The *Leadership* Spotlight." Remember, while your team is hoping for your success, if for no other reason that it makes their lives significantly more rewarding, they will also be watching you!

As a leader, it is your responsibility to take the first step in terms of *trust*, just as it is to take that step for *commitment*. After an appropriate period of observation, you may have a sincere desire to make changes to the way things are done by your team. While making changes for the sake of change is the wrong motivation, there is nothing wrong with you having your own ideas about how to improve the functioning of your team. That is exactly your purpose. It seems simple enough. Take charge, do the right thing and publish and disseminate the changes that you feel are needed.

Once they are introduced, however, be careful. It is

necessary for you to focus your attention on the execution of the changes you desire. Now is no time to go "wobbly" (Thank you Margaret Thatcher!) It may take a while for the changes to become reflexive for your team, but that doesn't mean you and your **leadership** team should not keep an eye out for violations of the new policy. Be prepared to correct those violations immediately through appropriate coaching.

Just as you are watching and enforcing, your team will be watching you. Now is the time that you must exercise self- discipline and self-**leadership** by setting the example to those whom you lead. If you set a policy to be at work at a specific time, then you must be aware that also applies to you. In fact, without being there prior to the designated time, you will find it impossible to recognize the achievers and correct those whose behavior needs adjustment. Do as I say, not as I do is not even a concept that belongs in quotes because there is absolutely no place in the **leadership** puzzle, or life in general, where it applies in the least!

WHAT DOES IT MATTER, NOBODY IS LOOKING?

As a team leader, you will be expected to display honor and integrity at every turn. Remember the statement that a leader is a leader 24/7? It never becomes more important than in dealing with honor. The hope is that as a person you have already figured out that living with a core value of honor just makes everything in life a lot easier. It's easier to sleep at night and easier to perform your mirror routine in the morning while you look yourself in the eye. If nothing else, with honor you never have to remember what the last fib was you told to make the next one make sense.

Calvin Coolidge said:

"The right thing to do never requires any subterfuge; it is always simple and direct."

(I am thinking that it may be useful if I stopped using dead presidents to make my points.)

With the examples of Bernie Madoff, Lance Armstrong, Barry Bonds and David Petraeus in mind, let me provide an example that never sees the headlines, occurs daily and makes the point better than any of the above examples.

Let's suppose your office has a very nicely appointed break room. There is a state of the art coffee machine, subsidized snacks and a place for folks to kick back for a few minutes to recharge their batteries. Your staff was so grateful to you for creating this space, they presented you with a ceramic coffee mug, with the words "WORLD'S BEST BOSS" printed on the side in gold leaf. Framed and hung on the wall near the sink is the sign that appears in virtually every break room in America: "Clean up after yourself. Your mother doesn't work here!" The problem is, you are the boss and cleaning your distinct coffee mug when you have had your last cup of the day seems like just a bit of busy work for an individual of your esteemed position. As a result, you avoid using the personalized mug in favor of one of the generic mugs in the cabinet. That way you can just leave it in the sink when you know no one is around and someone else with less stature in the organization will clean it for you. President Coolidge just offered you a solid piece of advice in identifying the right thing to do. Maybe dead presidents do provide useful lessons! If you are weighing several varied courses of action, consider this: which of your options would you be willing to defend to your children, those who appointed you and most importantly to that face of yours in the mirror tomorrow morning. That should help narrow down the options.

I'M WATCHING YOU, ALWAYS WATCHING

"Yeah, yeah, yeah. Set the example." If anyone in a *leadership* role didn't hear that on Day One, they weren't paying attention. "Don't worry. If anybody **is** in the break room, I always wash my own coffee cup! The darn gold leaf prevents me from sticking it in the dishwasher." Setting an example is a funny thing. It is inextricably linked to the concept of honor. Just about every quotable source in the history of the world with any credence has uttered something to the effect of "Honor is the way you behave when nobody is looking." Maybe there is a reason that all those sources chose to state a similar sentiment. That is because it is true and the gremlin that flips off the room light to throw you into "The *Leadership* Spotlight" has a transgression of honor first on his list of things to watch for. Gremlin? Relax. You two will soon become acquainted in "The *Leadership* Spotlight" chapter.

RULE 14: DO THE RIGHT THING

I previously mentioned that General Schwarzkopf listed this as one of his primary rules of *leadership*. As spoken, it's a pretty simple concept, so let's look at it in a bit more depth.

Of all the quotes in this book from war heroes, business leaders, dead presidents and even entertainers, I believe one of the most significant that relates to Rule 14 comes from one of my colleagues. When I first heard my colleague present the thought that "*Leadership* means being able to choose to do the **hard right** versus the **easy wrong**," it was in an environment that made the statement even more memorable:

A regional manager was conducting a small meeting. His intention was to rationalize the changing of the parameters for a sales contest in which we were all engaged. Without boring you with the details, the short version of it was the contest had been poorly conceived. Publication of the rules had failed to consider certain factors that were somewhat difficult to measure by the sales operations people who were administering the contest. Mind you, those factors were difficult to measure, not impossible. With a little added expense as well as some additional elbow grease by the analysts in sales, the contest awards could have been presented as originally planned. Instead, due to the extra effort required, the factors that determined the winners were altered and as a result, the winners of the contest were changed. In effect, the folks upstairs decided to move the goal line a little farther away and throw in a few extra plays that didn't happen. The result for the prospective winners was similar to this football analogy: Instead of leading by one point and having the ball with a first down and goal to go on the opponent's one yard line with thirty seconds left in the game, you are instead faced with a fourth down and goal to go from the twenty-five-yard line with only three seconds left. A touchdown would now be required for the win. Certainly, victory was achievable, but the challenge then became significantly more daunting.

As you might expect, the explanation from the regional manager was not popular. Corporate had been very vocal about the need for open and honest communication moving both ways through the chain of command, and to his credit, he was certainly open and honest. My friend felt that there was no time like the present to test the theory of openness and honesty being a two-way street. Being a former Army officer, she knew how to present her ideas with tact. Being a Texan, she also knew how to kick cow pies out of her way. (What surprised me was how well she could redirect one of those cow pies in heels!) So, with the utmost of that Texas Tact (a trait of hers I envy to this day) she raised her hand, and when called upon by the regional manager, her words echoed through the silence that followed:

"Sir, with all due respect, when you are in any leadership position, it is incumbent upon the leader to be able to recognize the hard right versus the easy wrong. The hard right is always the preferred course of action! May I respectfully recommend that if you are going to change the rules in the fourth quarter, you crack open the budget and recognize all of the winners under both sets of rules?"

In recalling the **leadership** choices that I have had to face in the past, I can only say that truer words were never spoken. When you examine the potential courses of action for your team, it is astounding how often your decision comes down to two choices. Frequently, one will seem like a "No Brainer" while the other is fraught with unfavorable consequences and difficulties such as the fear of undesirable precedents being set and extra work involved for all. It would be so much simpler to choose the "No Brainer" option. Be careful. Your options are not far from the maxim that says "If it is too good to be true, it probably isn't." In **leadership** situations, that can be translated to "The course of action that appears the easiest is rarely the best option in terms of either mission accomplishment or welfare of your people."

EVERYTHING I NEEDED TO KNOW ABOUT TRUST, I LEARNED ON DAY ONE! (ALMOST)

Demonstrating that you *trust* your team can and should begin as early as Day One. Unfortunately, in many situations it seems to go downhill from there, progressing into such heinous behaviors as the dreaded micromanagement monster. (They may be short, but they are irritating little beasts!)

Let's say that a new organization has just been formed. You are appointed to lead the team and successfully accomplish a mission that you cannot possibly accomplish on your own. The specific scenario involved is irrelevant. You could be a teacher in front of a classroom on the first day of school. Maybe you are a coach in front of her team immediately following the announcement of those selected for that team. Perhaps you are a sales manager introducing yourself to a newly hired group of sales professionals. As discussed in *commitment*, you will want to avoid making wholesale changes at this point, but it will be necessary for you to establish some rudimentary parameters to get things started. As a teacher, you might inform your students about your beginning class bell policy. Do you want them in the door by the time the bell rings or are they to be sitting at their desks? A coach may want to explain when practice begins for the team. If it is 4:30 p.m., what does 4:30 mean? Are they to arrive by 4:30? Be dressed in uniform at 4:30 or is 4:30 when you blow the whistle to begin warm ups? Your parameters are your first step in demonstrating *commitment*. Your next step is your first example of *trust*.

Let's allow a sales manager to bring this example to life:

"Welcome aboard! I hope you are as excited to be on this new team as I am to have you—yada, yada, yada. Before I close with a motivational comment that will make John Wooden turn over in his grave, let me address some housekeeping details. We begin work here at 8:30 a.m. That means to you that you are to be at your desk, ready to interact with clients at 8:25 a.m. If you are a coffee drinker, have it poised and ready to caffeinate you."

Now with that said, she has demonstrated what *commitment* she expects and she *trusts* them to honor that *commitment:* specifically, to be ready to work at 8:25 a.m. That should be simple enough, but wait! Since they probably don't sleep in the office, they will need to wake up at some point. Will she be there to ensure they set the alarm correctly? It is unlikely they will awake dressed and ready for work, so how can she be sure they will perform the personal hygiene procedure that will keep them from becoming an irritating colleague to the person at the next desk? Here it is, Day One and she has assigned a mission, yet she has not specified exactly how that mission is to be accomplished. She has issued no guidance as to when they should wake up to be at work on time. Standards of dress may have been addressed but she certainly won't be present in the employee's closet to choose which garments will be the most comfortable to ensure maximum productivity. With nothing else said, she has just exhibited effective *leadership.* She has demonstrated what commitment she expects and has shown that she *trusts* her people to live up to that *commitment.* (Is an image of effective and inspirational *leadership* beginning to form for you from the puzzle pieces?)

A major element of *trust* in effective *leadership* is the art of assigning someone a task to accomplish. This includes specifying any absolute requirements, clarifying any questions they have. Combine that with ensuring they have the skills and understanding to accomplish the task. Now get out of the way! The act of supervising without micromanaging to see how they are coming along, i.e. being at the office before 8:25 a.m. to see who arrives on time is called follow-up. It is necessary and will be covered thoroughly in the next chapter.

As you are observing your team work, you will have the opportunity to see the learning potential of a decision point. In your own experience, you possibly may have encountered the same crossroads that your people are coming upon. You must fight the impulse to jump in and direct their decision in these circumstances. Just because you took a different path in your decision process, does not have to necessarily infer that another individual's skill set will not translate to success on a path that you may have overlooked.

Does this mean that an effective leader can never shortstop a significant error that a rookie is about to make? Absolutely not! What it does mean is that in this instance you should examine the consequences of the potential error. Will it significantly hinder the progress towards mission accomplishment? Will blood be involved? Will the impending error become obvious quickly? Will correction be easy and at the same time will it provide a learning point?

My wife, Beth and I have lived in our home town for two decades. We have both spent many years in sales in our community, so we know the roads well. Frequently we will be traveling to a destination that we could both get to independently in two separate cars, taking two different routes in about the same elapsed time. Over the years, we have learned that it is best when one of us is the passenger to keep their opinions about route selection to themselves. If Beth is driving to the home of one of our children, I need to realize that she knows how to get there even if it is not the route I would have chosen and vice versa. Is there an exception? There certainly is. Let's say she is navigating while I drive, and she has pulled up traffic patterns on her smart phone. As a result, Beth sees that Arapahoe Road is bumper to bumper traffic, and taking that route, which is my favorite, will make us late. The learning opportunity of not taking that road between 4:00 p.m. and 6:00 p.m. is now superseded by the fact that if she doesn't suggest I recalculate to the interstate and take Parker Road., we will be stuck in traffic. That would potentially be a mistake which will significantly delay our expected arrival time, irritating our daughter and generally making a mess of the evening.

AS A WINGMAN, YOU NEVER, EVER LEAVE YOUR LEAD

In a previous organization in which I served as a manager, the standard issue item for a new leader was a high quality, name brand pen and pencil set. Never have I come across an organization that issues a red cape with a big yellow "S" on the back of it to newly appointed leaders. When you are eventually appointed to an esteemed *leadership* position, no one expects you to be perfect 24/7. But you must remember you are a leader 24/7. There will be times of disappointment. You will screw up. You will be tasked with what seems to be the impossible, and you will be required to promulgate orders that make absolutely no sense to you whatsoever. It is critical that you understand that the worst mistake you can make in these situations is to vent your frustration, disappointment; self-esteem issues etc. to the **wrong** person… particularly to someone on your team.

Every leader, to maintain their sanity, their perspective as well as their sense of humor needs to have someone who they can talk to in confidence. In the aviation community, this individual is known as a **wingman**. In a two-plane flight, one pilot will have lead and the other will be the wingman. It is the wingman's job to protect the lead so he can focus on the primary target without fear of being caught by surprise by a hostile aircraft coming from below or behind. In some circles, it has become common to refer to the buddy who goes to the bar with you (who ironically, has similar duties to that real wingman) as your wingman. In selecting your wingman, exercise caution.

First let's talk about whom is **not** an ideal wingman:

1. A wingman should never be junior to you in rank. Remember 24/7?

2. A wingman should never be a potential rival for your job. What happens in Vegas doesn't stay in Vegas when it comes to corporate advancement.

3. A wingman should not be senior to you

So, who makes a good a wingman?

1. A peer who understands your duties and frustrations. A manager in the information technology field will not be particularly useful to a high school teacher as a wingman, due simply to a lack of appreciation for each other's jobs.

2. Someone who is not afraid to set you straight when fatigue has made you view reality with a skewed perspective. If you aren't considering the need for mission accomplishment as well as the

welfare of your people, your wingman must be prepared to summon you back to reality and quickly. If not, they would be doing you a disservice by putting lipstick on a pig. They should appreciate the problem, but at the same time assist you in identifying a solution.

3. Remember the example of the ride to the airport in the chapter on **Commitment**? The buddy who gave up his party to make sure you got to the plane on time is a prime candidate for the honored title of wingman. Of course, if you are considering elevating him to a wingman role, be prepared to play that role for him or her as well!

WOMEN IN *LEADERSHIP: TRUST*

For a woman in a *leadership* role, the concept of setting the example to generate *trust* can take on added challenges as well as opportunities. Human nature being what it is, it can be difficult for some people (men or women) to be led by a woman. That feeling certainly isn't appropriate, but it never the less exists. Call it a macho thing or possibly simple gender jealousy. Women who assume *leadership* roles can sometimes take on a more difficult journey. Take heart. If you can get past the "B" word (yes, it will rear its ugly head during the *trust* discussion) you will be presented with a tremendous opportunity as well.

Perhaps the fact that men can face similar challenges when they are working in previously female dominated roles may just make the challenge easier to overcome. In occupations that are primarily staffed my members of specific genders, the expectations to set the example are often set lower for a new leader of a different gender by the rank and file. It frequently is not even a conscious diminishment of expectations, but a simple outdated relic of the American culture. Consider the challenges faced by a male kindergarten teacher, or a female fireman.

At one point in time it was considered appropriate for women to "go first." Let me paint a *leadership* example of that concept not working out so well:

At a recently held corporate meeting, the manager was a woman. For lunch that day the team was served a buffet style meal in the main lodge away from the meeting room. For one of the few times in corporate life, the meeting broke early and the attendees arrived at the private lunch room a few minutes before the buffet was prepared for service.

In every leadership scenario that exists, it is sacrosanct that the leaders eat last. This is a behavior that applies to taking care of your people before you worry about yourself. The practical reason is that if there is enough for all to eat, it all works out fine. However, if the amount served is less than required for the entire team, or events conspire to interrupt lunch, the leader will be assured that their team has had the opportunity to be nourished. This meeting took place in a major resort hotel so the chances of a food shortage were minimal. (In 2002, at the Park City Olympics however, several venues ran out of hot dogs, so don't think that it can't happen at the Ritz Carlton in Maui.) Perhaps that is why our manager's eyes lit up as she exclaimed, "Great! Lunch is here! I'm starving!" Grabbing a plate, she then led us through the buffet. Maybe it was hunger which elevated a more basic need above the welfare of her team. Maybe she just wasn't thinking. You can correctly assume that the number of individuals in her team that executed the "Are you kidding me?" eye roll at her faux pas was a majority, consisting of both males and females.

In the example, the transgression was not due to the confusion of gender roles but simple to a lack of **leadership** awareness. The manager had most likely been exposed to a "ladies first" consideration in her past, and failed to let *leadership* considerations take precedence in this situation. While some might consider those attitudes condescending, one must admit, some were beneficial. With women's equality coming on rapidly in many circles, what was formerly thought of as "good manners" that are applied in social settings when a woman is present are not meant as insults or a denigration of any kind. Neither are they appropriate reasons to ignore *leadership* principles. They just may not be appropriate in a professional setting anymore. As a woman, don't expect them in business. Should they be observed by someone inappropriately, yet with good intentions, consider history and make a corrective adjustment as required.

For any leader to roll up their sleeves, or throw on a pair of overalls and lend a hand to gain a perspective on what the actual job requirements of their teammates are can only serve to surprise, impress and elevate their status in *leadership* roles.

Once you have spent enough time getting an understanding of what that task requires and have had the chance to do it yourself, thank your tour guide for the opportunity, jump out of the ditch or climb down from the scaffolding, remove the overalls and clean the gunk from your hands. Resume your role as a leader and I can assure you that the next time any derogatory word gets used around those with whom you have set the example; you will likely be defended vociferously by those that were in the ditch with you. At the very least, the offending individual will not have a sympathetic ear listening to them.

TRUST: THE FIRST STEP

In the event, you read this book in its entirety, you will come close to being able to recite this section by heart. That is because it will appear more than once as the conclusion to a chapter, if only one chapter is deemed pertinent to be read at any one time.

I describe the *leadership* relationship as being like any personal relationship. Two of the three primary qualities of a leader, *commitment* and now *trust* are vital to any relationship. They are critical in a romantic relationship, a family relationship, a sales relationship or a platonic relationship. When all three are present, the relationship is at its peak. Remove one element, and the relationship can still function, just not at as high of a level. Remove two elements and any relationship is at serious risk of failing. For all the factors thus far identified, it is up to the leader to **take the first step**.

You have the benefit of information your teammates do not have. When you bring on new team members, you have the responsibility of ensuring they know what is expected of them. That may mean covering it more than once and in more than one fashion. Communication is a command responsibility. It is simply not acceptable for any of your teammates to ever say with sincerity, "I had no idea that was expected of me." It is understood that people can use that excuse to shirk responsibility, but if a lack of communication is what caused the shortfall, the responsibility falls directly on the leader.

The element of *trust* can be a deceptive one. It is your responsibility to set an example so your team will see that the standards you have communicated in your *commitment* stance are worthwhile. They must pertain to the mission or the welfare of your team. If the standard does not pertain to either, then it very well may be irrelevant. If it is too minor for even you to follow, even when no one is looking, it is most likely irrelevant or unworthy of your team's effort to observe as well.

RICHARD BROWN

CARING

"He has a right to criticize who has
a heart to help."

--Abraham Lincoln

"I have yet to find the man, however exalted his
station, who did not do betterwork and put forth
greater effort under a spiritof approval than under
a spirit ofcriticism."

--Charles Schwab

119

RICHARD BROWN

CARING

While one might consider the new Manager's tenure as a sales representative brief, he felt his four years in the field had allowed him to gain a comprehensive picture of the requirements of a sales manager during his four years selling in the field. Combined with his military leadership experience, he agreed with his managers that he was ready to lead a sales district of ten seasoned representatives. The sales job had always been fun for him. In his view, eighty percent of the requirement was simply showing up with the other twenty percent being able to effectively communicate the advantages of his products succinctly, accurately and passionately to his customers. He was certain that he had a solid grasp on what it would take for him to help his new team achieve unprecedented levels of success. His first major lesson to be learned lurked right around the corner.

His new team was as diverse as the new

Manager expected. Several members had been with the company for decades. Some were relatively recently hired but still had a few years of experience under their belts.

The individual who was central to this situation had been in his territory for thirteen years. Aaron was well liked by his colleagues and his clients as well as being a joy to work with. During sales training meetings when the representatives would hone their product message with the new strategies designed by the marketing department, Aaron was a blessing. His ability to assimilate a new strategy and to communicate it effectively in front of his peers in a role play situation was a significant benefit to the Manager. To perfect their verbiage, all the representatives would utilize "sticky notes" to help them learn the new points of emphasis. Aaron would attach these to the pages of his visual aid for support as his colleagues did. It wasn't long before he had the points committed to memory so that the yellow rectangular pieces of paper were an unnecessary afterthought.

The fact that Aaron could be relied upon to give an excellent presentation to his peers provided the Manager with a useful example of "how it should be done." As a result, the

Manager didn't have to be the only one to give a demonstration of what was expected. Anytime a peer can support a strategy, it adds significantly to the credibility of the message from the manager. Aaron was perfectly suited for that role.

Outside of meetings, the Manager spent a significant amount of time on field rides observing the representatives during their interaction with customers. The Manager had not lived anywhere near Aaron's territory during his own time in the field, so every day was an adventure for him, exploring the suburbs of the city and getting to know his team. Field rides were always a joy with Aaron. His customers were happy to see him and they welcomed him into their offices, even though there was no scheduled appointment. His presentations to his customers did have a different feel than the "silver tongued" professional who could captivate a room full of his peers at a meeting. While his product presentation was as comprehensive as ever, there were rarely any objections raised by the customer. Impromptu sales discussions regarding tangents to the main presentation rarely took place, as happened during field rides with other reps. When Aaron held his visual aid to show data supporting his statements, his hands trembled *more than you would expect from a thirteen-year veteran.*

While reviewing past performance records of his new team, the Manager noticed a disturbing pattern regarding Aaron. Despite his apparent proficiency at the job, Aaron could not be described as particularly successful. In fact, in recent years, he had won none of the frequent contests that help motivate the more materialistic personalities of sales people. His salary increases, primarily based upon merit, had been minimal. In fact, his salary was even below that of representatives with significantly less tenure due to his mediocre sales results. Within a year of the Manager's arrival, he scheduled a standard field ride with Aaron. They would visit Aaron's customers with a new product discussion a shortly after the most recent sales meeting. The Manager liked to give seasoned representatives a few days to become familiar with the new approach before facing the pressure of working with the boss. The field ride with Aaron was scheduled for two full weeks after the meeting ended.

The day arrived and as they made their way around the territory, the adventure of exploring new areas was no longer present for the young

Manager. In fact, he noticed that several of the customers that Aaron planned on seeing that day had been the same ones they visited during their last field ride. As they began their product discussion with the first client, Aaron pulled out his visual aid to display a graph of study data. There, like a flag on every page, was the canary yellow sticky note that had been used as a tool at the meeting two weeks earlier. At the end of their time with the client, she remarked to Aaron that it was great to see him, even if he did "Show up earlier than I had expected you to be here."

Even to the "wet behind the ears" Manager, it was obvious that he now faced a leadership challenge. Aaron's commitment to the goal obviously was not what he had portrayed. The presence of the yellow sticky notes was a red flag, and an indication that Aaron may not have made any calls on clients for two full weeks between the meeting and the field ride. Even if he had worked, but failed to remove the notes, that fact severely damaged the trust that the Manager felt he could place in Aaron.

After the sales call, the Manager suggested that they go grab a cup of coffee. Now it was _his_ turn to earn the big bucks. Over coffee, the Manager probed Aaron regarding what was called a milk *run: set up visits with friendly clients that appear to be spontaneous calls on the day you worked with the boss. His visual aid, usually an inherent part of any product discussion, had apparently not been opened in two weeks or he would have noticed and removed the sticky notes from the meeting. Once each of these deficiencies was addressed, Aaron was given the opportunity to explain. No explanation was forthcoming, just as none was required. It was obvious. The reason for Aaron's lack of success in his job simply was because he wasn't working.*

The field day ended prematurely with a review of what was expected of Aaron in return for his salary. Prior to leaving, the Manager asked Aaron a question that had been nagging at him for the entire morning. "Aaron, have you ever considered taking up a different line of work?" Puzzled, Aaron responded, "No, I haven't. Why do you ask?" The Manager responded "In reviewing your career, it seems that your capabilities reflect greater potential than does your performance." With that, the two went their separate ways with a plan to meet again the following week with a better performance expected from Aaron.

During the rest of the week, while the Manager considered his next step, he was puzzled as to why someone who had the capability to succeed chose not to perform as expected. As related previously, in the Manager's mind, this job really wasn't that difficult. Certainly, a man of Aaron's capability should be able to succeed if he just went to work.

As the morning of the follow up field ride with Aaron dawned, the two met at the usual spot. Uncharacteristically, this time it was Aaron who asked if they could talk over a cup of coffee. Before the coffee stopped jiggling from the server placing it in front of them, Aaron informed his Manager that he had decided to resign from the company. He had received an offer to train as a financial analyst, an area that Aaron enjoyed discussing as much as his Manager enjoyed discussing sports. As he revealed his decision, a significant event took place. It appeared that a huge weight had been lifted from Aaron's shoulders.

After completing the protocol required in such a situation, the Manager asked if he could ask Aaron a question. "Now that it's done, how do you feel?" "Boss", he said, "You can't imagine how relieved I am and at the same time how excited I am for the future!" Aaron had been laboring with a cross to bear that the new

Manager had no idea was even possible for a man of his talents. Aaron simply did not enjoy the job and had not enjoyed it for years. Going to work every day was an ever-increasing burden. Now that he had shed that burden, he couldn't stop smiling. Then he said something else that gave the Manager a critical puzzle piece. "Thank you! Thank you for caring enough about me to analyze my career. Thank you for caring enough to suggest that I might be happier and more successful doing something else! By the way, my wife asked me to thank you as well and to give you a big hug. She has experienced the same sense of relief as I, but can we just shake hands and call it even?"

At first blush, it might seem obvious that **caring** would be one of the four corner puzzle pieces with which to start construction of the **leadership** image. I have defined **leadership** as getting someone to do something that **you** want done because **they** want to do it. As such, that "someone" would seem to be a critical factor in the equation. After all, without people, how is any team supposed to accomplish their objective? Well, that is only a part of the equation. Any competent manager knows that if a job requires ten people to accomplish it, then showing up with nine is going to present a challenge.

What I want to address is *caring* from a more expansive perspective than a table of organization. While it is that humans make up your team, your class or your organization of any type, the secret to success is remembering that they are more than just a means to an end. They are people as well. Their lives extend beyond the fraction of the day they spend helping you achieve what you want done. They have signed on to your organization. It is imperative that you remember that success requires your relationship with them to be symbiotic. Just as much as you want to succeed as an organization, they want to succeed as individuals within that organization. The *commitment* that they expect from you is to help them do just that.

FRACTIONS, PERCENTAGES AND SUCCESS

There is a curious reality within an organization with regards to improving the performance of the group. Let's take for example a sales team like the one depicted in the opening scenario of this chapter. To improve the performance of the group you must focus your attention on each individual person in the group. Attempting to move the group as a single entity is futile. That approach ignores the reality that your team is made up of individuals. Those individuals have different goals and motivations. By treating them alike, you are doing nothing more productive than attempting to herd cats. Over time, you will begin to observe that your team will follow a common recipe.

Approximately twenty percent of the organization will be what we refer to as **water walkers**. These are the two out of ten who are going to be at the top of the performance ladder. Their motivation is sky high and they have a goal in mind. Whether it is making the All-Star Team, becoming the class valedictorian or earning a promotion to a *leadership* position, their performance will be difficult to impact negatively. Even with the least effective leader assigned to that group, these individuals will still perform well...up to a point. It is important to know that this top tier will not necessarily always be the same individuals. Remember, "Life is what happens before you clock in and after you clock out." It is entirely possible that what happens in their lives has the potential to affect their performance at work.

As a manager, I was fortunate to have many superstars on my sales team. The same existed in my infantry platoons and my baseball teams. I would like to introduce you to one of them. His first name is Paul.

For my first five years as a manager, he consistently

competed for highest honors in our region at the end of the year. Paul routinely led the district in sales. In my sixth year as his manager, he suffered an emotionally crippling personal loss that devastated him and destroyed the retirement dreams of he and his wife. In coping with the catastrophe his performance suffered. Instead of being in the top three in the region out of seventy-five, he finished fifteenth in the region and fourth in the district. (I only mention incidentally that *my* boss at the time was terribly disappointed that Paul had let a little thing like the complete destruction of their dream bed and breakfast under construction in a fire hinder his performance!)

While Paul wasn't in the top two of our district that year, someone else stepped up and filled that role. The second top spot rotated among one or two other individuals. In this instance, the performance of a member of the team obviously deteriorated due to issues unrelated to the work environment. It happens. It was incumbent upon me as his leader as well as my responsibility to the company to watch for his recovery. If it had been absent, then my role would be to offer the assistance and guidance required for that return to excellence. Thankfully, Paul returned to his previous levels of performance the following year. He was always there to make my job easier.

There is another twenty percent of the organization
that theoretically will demand eighty percent of your
time. Don't let them have it! This is the twenty
percent of the organization at the bottom. (At this
point I will ignore my proofreaders and expose my
infamous, yet adorable lack of tact. While anyone can
have a down year, if you put a few of those years
together in succession you become what may be
referred to as a **bottom dweller**.) In the district
example from above, this doesn't mean they will be in
the bottom twenty percent of the larger region, or
even be performing poorly. It means they simply will
be ranked in the bottom twenty percent of the team
that you lead. Again, it may not always be the same
two people, but there always will be a number nine
and ten on a ten-person team. Do not let relative
standing blur your vision regarding their performance.
If you are leading a ten-person team within a larger
team of eighty and your numbers nine and ten are
numbers eleven and twelve of the larger team, there
probably is not a lot of adjustment required. In the
same sense, if your numbers one and two are ranked
in the bottom twenty percent of the larger team and
everyone else is below them you do indeed have a
performance challenge.

So, we have twenty percent on the top, the **water
walkers**, and twenty percent on the bottom, or the

bottom dwellers. That accounts for forty percent of the team. What we are left with is the middle sixty percent. In keeping with my nickname pattern, I will call them the **backbone**… because they are. From time to time a few of them will pop into the top tier just as one or two may fall into the bottom tier. This **backbone** is the portion of your team you need to focus on the most. Let's say that the **backbone** ranks from thirty to sixty in a region of eighty. Through coaching, mentoring and leading, move the **backbone** upwards so they rank from twenty to fifty. With the same tools applied differently maintain your **water walkers** along with your **bottom dwellers** in their respective positions. Now you are going to be the team to beat.

GATHER 'ROUND THE CAMPFIRE

So much for the sheer numbers pertaining to *leadership*. *Leadership* is about people, remember? Management is about things. Numbers fit the definition of things. Besides, it is impossible to move the **backbone** up as a group. In our example of a ten-person district, sixty percent equates to six separate and distinct individuals. Those personalities are much more than cubbies in a mail room, numbers on a roster or names on a seating chart. They have chosen to remain in your organization for one of two simple reasons. They want to succeed or they just need a job. How much they want to succeed is for them to know and for you to find out. It is then your job to help them achieve their goal if the cumulative effect of those goals allows you to achieve the team goal. Don't obsess about your goals. That's your leader's job. As a leader, if you help your people get what they seek; your numbers will take care of themselves.

Some schools of thought believe and teach that it is up to leaders to motivate their people to move them individually up the ladder. I believe that people can't really motivate anyone other than themselves. The leader can provide the environment for others to motivate themselves, but the execution is up to the individual. Sales organizations that have instituted "open-ended" bonus plans (translated to mean you can earn as much as possible with no arbitrary cap on earnings) are surprised to learn that some individuals still perform below what is expected.

A wise, grizzled and grumpy Marine Corps Gunnery Sergeant demonstrated this principle to a group of officer candidates. He selected one poor soul to assist him with a demonstration about motivation and leadership. The Gunny laid a rope up the slope of a hill and told a "volunteer" to push the rope up the hill. As hard as the candidate tried, he was unsuccessful. The rope just gathered into a pile as the result of his pushing. Amidst profane and less than flattering (yet still hilarious) comments from the Gunny, the candidate volunteer returned the rope to its original position as directed. The Gunny then walked to the end of the rope that was uphill, picked it up and pulled it up the hill. Mission accomplished! The moral: leadership isn't pushing from the rear; it is leading from the front!

Do you feel I have used too many military examples? Okay, let's find something a little more commonplace. Think of your team as a campfire. With a little practice, some dry wood and appropriate kindling, it is not difficult to get a fire started. Once the kindling has flared and the logs catch, the fire can rapidly roar into a blaze that would back the devil up a few paces. Think of your **water walkers** as that roaring beginning of the campfire. You can be assured that its intensity will not remain constant over a long period, but not much needs to be done to it in the beginning. Your only concern should be to keep something in the immediate vicinity from catching fire unintentionally. (In the sales setting, you could only hope to be so lucky!) The similarity of a campfire to a team at this phase is simple. Stand back. Marvel at what you have created, but don't throw any more wood on it. Just admire the warmth!

As the fuel settles in, the fire will tone itself down to something that is appropriate for marshmallows and weenie roasts. This is the phase of the campfire that you want to remain constant for most the evening. Now is when the memories will be made. It is also now that maintenance begins to be required because the fire won't stay that way by itself.

A fire can stay perfect for campers if unattended for only a limited period. As logs are consumed and the structure of the fire shifts, new firewood may be required to maintain the intensity. Maybe now is the time to shift a few logs to give access to oxygen to keep the flame at that perfect stage. Your **backbone** equates to this stage of the fire. You don't want to ignore them in favor of improving the bottom tier. Too much tinkering and trying to motivate all of them to be **water walkers,** at this point, will be counterproductive. Consider that to be just like pushing around the logs in the fire pit; too much at this point will mess up what you have already created. With a little constructive adjustment and some additional motivational environment, it is more than possible to take some of them into the top tier, if **they** desire to put in the effort.

At the end of the evening and when the log pile has

all but disappeared, the intensity of the fire will die down. While it would be possible to cut up a tree for more wood, it is a challenging task to regenerate the beautiful dancing flame of previous hours. This phase equates to your **bottom dwellers**. Just like the fire that has diminished because of a lack of fuel or too much prodding and poking, your bottom tier performers may be there for a lack of fuel as well (or more appropriately a lack of motivation). It is important in this phase to provide the action that is required to allow the fire to take the appropriate course. Maybe that means it is time to extinguish the flame and head off to the tents. It is certainly not appropriate to ignore the fire and let it chart its own course unattended throughout the night.

For your **bottom dwellers**, particularly if they are routinely the **bottom dwellers**, an analysis of their motivation level as well as their proper fit for the job is required as was the case in the example featuring Aaron. Maybe their heart just isn't in the work any longer, and a change in career path is appropriate. They may have exceeded their competency level, but remain in their jobs because it is more comfortable to remain and not perform. Making a career change may not be an option that they relish. This is usually due to a lack of appropriate feedback from their leader. Possibly, life has dealt them a wild card and in addition to dealing with your demands, they are facing insurmountable obstacles outside of work that are keeping them from performing adequately. An effective leader will make the effort to discover which is the case. Whatever the reason, just like a fading campfire at the end of the evening, they should not be ignored, nor should you try to recreate the roaring blaze that you had at the beginning in the blink of an eye.

WHAT IS YOUR MISSION?

When I was the leader of a ten-person sales district, my boss and I had a little inside joke. While discussing goals, I would tell him that I was working for a free week off. Our national division had an award trip for the top ten percent of performers in each region. Among other rewards, the winning representatives and their guests would receive an invitation to attend an all-expense paid trip to a resort location. While challenging to say the least, it was numerically possible for every one of my representatives to win this award. Should they all win? Then I would have nothing to do for the entire week they were gone, save paperwork. Because of my team's absence my boss could not make me take vacation time! (For some reason, this was not the only time his tough Texas personality failed to appreciate my California sense of humor!)

While it was possible for every one of my charges to be award winners, it was not probable and that was not my mission. My district was expected to exceed my assigned quota. That was the mission I was assigned by corporate when I accepted the job. The district quota was an aggregate of all the territory quotas that made up my district. I was not required to send everyone on the award trip.

My **water walkers** were the ones who earned the award trips. I cheered them on and stood by to provide any assistance that they might desire. If the **backbone** were all exceeding their quota, I spent my time poking and prodding (remember the fire?) to the degree necessary to keep their fire burning well. When required I would throw another log onto the fire to maintain its intensity. If the **backbone** exceeded their quota, I was happy. If they wanted to shift into high gear and asked me to pour a little lighter fluid on them to ignite them to the next level for the award trip, I was ready to help them. I had no right or desire to demand that they put in the time and effort to be a **water walker** if they were not motivated for the *commitment* that was involved. The performance of the **water walkers** and the **backbone** in this scenario would be enough to cover our district requirement to exceed quota. If the **bottom dwellers** were also exceeding quota, the district mission of meeting quota at the end of the year may have been accomplished by the end of November!

BECOMING THE ANSWER TO THE QUESTION

Let's revisit our definition of *leadership*. The ability to get someone to accomplish something that **you** want done because **the**y want to do it. To see within a person's psyche to determine if they did something because they wanted to or not is an impossible task. As a result, *leadership* endeavors are frequently evaluated simply on the successful completion of the task at hand. Rarely are those individuals that completed the task queried as to what made them do it.

With that definition in mind, we could almost fold the tent at this point and move to the next town. But the title of this book is not "Become a Successful Leader." Instead it is "Become THE LEADER Your PEOPLE DESERVE." Thus, we are about to embark on the difference between an <u>effective</u> leader and an <u>inspirational</u> leader.

I have discovered an interesting phenomenon while discussing *leadership* with others. Frequently these discussions take place at networking events, read "cocktail parties." Usually I am trying to wrestle with a small plate of bacon wrapped scallops, crudités, and an elusive meatball or two while balancing an adult beverage at the same time. I have found that if I can get other people talking, I can focus on the task at hand. (This of course is listening to them while trying to capture the meatball without spilling the beverage.) In this situation, whenever I have posed a specific question, "Who was your most memorable boss, coach, or teacher?" I have rarely found anyone who can't immediately recall one specific individual. Usually the full name of that individual is stated before the echoes of the original question have dissipated. Timing is everything. When I ask the question, I don't eat anything until I ask a follow up question: "Why is that person the one you remember over all of the other possibilities?" Now I can enjoy that bacon wrapped scallop. I should have some time to chew and listen!

The interesting thing about that little cocktail party forum is by the time we reach the age of appropriate attendance at cocktail parties, we have had countless teachers, coaches and probably at least a few bosses. Despite that, rarely is there more than one or maybe two names given as the answer to the question. Someone stands out! Usually it is only one memorable former leader above all others. That leader probably wasn't the only one who would have been able to get the team to accomplish their assigned mission. So, what made my cocktail party conversation partner tell me their story, or recall that example as the answer to the question?

When pressed to explain what made that leader memorable the answer is usually not "Because we accomplished what we set out to do." Chances are most of the teams did accomplish their goal. That may be what keeps a leader in the job, but it's not what makes them memorable, sometimes thirty years after the fact. Most often, that impact was because of something special, something unique, something life-changing the leader provided to that individual. Maybe it was because "She challenged me to exceed what I expected of myself, and I achieved it." Or it is something like: "We were more than just a group to him. He took an interest in all of us as individuals." I have even heard, "I'm not sure, but there was just something about the way she worked that made me want to put out extra effort. In turn, that helped me succeed and contributed to a great team performance as well."

As I reminisce about my most memorable leaders, a significant thread comes to mind. The ones who groomed me as a leader all had a common philosophy expressed in various ways: "While accomplishing your goals through the actions of your team, remember that many leaders can get the mission accomplished. That is only half of your job. The other half of your job pertains to the welfare of the individuals on your team. In the military, this is easy to see. In business, where life and death situations rarely occur, your opportunity to look out for their welfare comes largely from your desire to **develop** your people!"

The *commitment* to encourage greater personal development, while getting the job done, is what can make you the "answer to the question" thirty years later at a cocktail party. That development may entail uncovering motivation, adjusting behavior to meet expectations, encouraging success or in Aaron's case, helping to clear the trees so one can see the forest.

SMALL BATCH BOURBON FOR MY HORSES

A basic truth in *leadership* is that if there is behavior you want repeated, it must be reinforced. (Undesirable behavior may also end up being repeated if it is mishandled and reinforced. Remember, to some people, negative attention is better than no attention at all.) A major responsibility of a leader is to recognize and reinforce desirable behavior. Ideally, reinforcing positive behavior is done in a public setting. Negative behavior should be adjusted in a private setting whenever possible. In this way leaders not only accomplish their missions, but develop the people on their team as well. Frequently this principle is referred to as providing positive or negative feedback. The first thing you might want to do is to discard those semantics.

One could make the case that the same feedback always has the potential to be either beneficial or negative, depending upon how it is delivered. "Nice hat!" could also be delivered as "Nice to see you wear a hat that doesn't embarrass all of us, Knucklehead!" These are the same messages, but they generate two completely different responses. The reality is, positive reinforcement of behavior is certainly useful in a *leadership* role. That reinforcement runs second, however, to the utility of constructive, accurate feedback coupled with appropriate coaching to imprint a desired behavior. (My sense is that I am verging on the academic, which is something I promised I would not do in this book.)

The **least expensive, most effective** method to reinforce positive behavior (and ideally getting more of it) is simply to tell the individual responsible what you have seen them accomplish and that you appreciate the efforts that resulted in whatever it was that they did. In other words; "Catch them doing something…right." Be specific!! "Nice job on that report!" is a warm fuzzy, but it doesn't reinforce the specific features of the teammate's behavior that impressed you.

Frequently the business world gets all wrapped up in material rewards for a job well done. Because I was one, I can attest that sales folk tend to fall on the materialistic side of this issue. Goodies for a job well done are nice, but at the same time, the biggest rewards were not always the most meaningful.

One of the most memorable mementos of appreciation I ever received came from a Vice President of Sales. Upon completion of a year's performance that placed you in the top tier, you would receive a letter on corporate letterhead, signed by The VP of sales himself. It came with a handwritten, personalized note from the VP congratulating you on your performance and wishing you continued success in the year to come. Certainly, a nice gesture, but for this corporate titan of a Fortune 100 company to take the time to write an individual note on each of the letters that were sent out was kind of a big deal. It wasn't a long note, more along the lines of "Great performance this year, Rick! I appreciate all you do to drive your district's efforts! Have a halcyon year next year!" ("Halcyon" was his trademark adjective.) Those letters are still close at hand, while my plaques and trophies are in a box in my storage locker. I can't say for certain that those notes had the same effect on everybody, but I know for certain how they helped me motivate myself for next year.

Don't get me wrong. Trips to St. John and engraved plaques have their place in the world of kudos and Atta boys, but an expensive token to say "I appreciate what you do!" is not always necessary. What has always been just a bit perplexing to me is that by its very nature, positive feedback, praise or a pat on the back, should be an enjoyable experience for everyone involved. Remember- praise is the least expensive, most effective way to reinforce desired behavior. As such, I must wonder why it is utilized so infrequently.

What about "negative feedback"? Well **that** certainly doesn't sound like any fun at all! So, let's modify that phrase. Accurate feedback phrased tactfully is always useful. It simply makes us better at whatever it is we are trying to accomplish. When we describe it as "negative", it is understandable that it might be something to be avoided. The problem is, if your team is trying to accomplish something and one of the team members is not doing what is required of them, it is going to be more difficult to get the goal achieved. To correct the shortfall, something is going to have to be said to the individual not carrying their share of the load. If that is not done, either the team comes up short or everyone else must pick up more than their share. Remember those "big bucks" we discussed? This is where you earn them. You might even consider these situations worth half of your salary. Why? Because if all you had to do was to dish out praise and rewards for jobs well done, they would not have to pay you anywhere near as much as they do! Relax. We can make the task actually enjoyable.

The first thing we need to do is rebrand this activity so it doesn't sound so onerous. If "negative feedback" or "corrective action" makes you want to shy away from helping someone do a better job, consider calling it a "constructive adjustment." However, you label it, remember, this is how you help people develop their skills and become more successful. This is how you hold team members to account. If the process of identifying the need for constructive adjustment and taking the required action is not comfortable for you, you should go back to the foundations of why you are in a *leadership* position in the first place. Again, I would ask "why do you want to lead?" Being willing to do <u>this</u> is how you become the answer to the question!

THREE REASONS BUT A MILLION EXCUSES

When you are leading people to accomplish a goal, there is a simple reality to remember. There are only three reasons people don't do what they are expected to do:

1. They didn't know they were supposed to do it.

If we are dealing with #1, then the solution is incredibly simple. **You** need do a better job communicating! Communication is always a <u>command</u> responsibility. It is up to the leader to make sure everyone on the team knows what is expected of them for satisfactory performance. Saying it once may be enough, but it may not be. <u>Failure is not an option</u> here. You must make sure your team knows what is expected of them. How do you know if they are aware? Have them tell you or show you what <u>they</u> think <u>you</u> expect of them. If their response is correct, it is an opportunity for positive reinforcement. In the event their perception does not match your expectation, it is up to you to either correct the perception or adjust the expectation.

2. They didn't know how to do it.

Coaching, rehearsal, practice, whatever you want to call it, is an important part of *leadership*. Even those with prior experience at a similar task in another organization may fall woefully short of the standards in your organization simply because it is a different organization. Abraham Lincoln said, "Give me six hours to chop down a tree and I will spend the first four hours sharpening the axe!" SEAL Team Six spent countless hours rehearsing the takedown of Osama Bin Laden in 2012. Apollo astronauts Armstrong, Aldrin and Collins rehearsed the Apollo 11 moon landing in 1969 until they could land on the moon in their sleep. Maybe your organization has more going for it than SEAL Team Six and the Apollo 11 crew, but it doesn't mean you don't have to provide coaching to your people.

3. **They didn't want to do it badly enough.**

In this case, you are dealing with a *commitment* issue. You know the million excuses that fall outside of the 3 reasons people don't do what they are supposed to? This is where those excuses come from. "I didn't have the right tools" translates to, "I didn't want to do it badly enough to manage to **get** the right tools." Remember the example of a ride to the airport? "Dude, I wanted to give you a ride, but my alarm didn't go off!" means, "I didn't want to do it badly enough to make sure I woke up with duplicate alarms." In this situation, you need to ensure that you can gain the *commitment* level you require. If not, it might be worth examining other options to fill the role of the less than committed player.

WHAT MOTIVATES YOU?

So how do you provide the environment to motivate people to help them improve their performance? Well it's complicated. **Ask them!** If they don't have an answer, your first job is to help them discover and develop a genuine motivation that will drive their efforts. As depicted in the example of the open- ended bonus plan, don't assume the answer is always money. In fact, history has shown that it rarely is the case. Motivation may come from recognition, potential for advancement, flexibility to be able to coach a little league baseball team after work or fighting like a "Devil Dog" to protect the guys in the infantry formation on either side of you. Once you discover <u>that</u> secret, you are well on your way to really knowing your people at work. Important, yes, but that's not enough. Don't forget about life.

As a sales manager, for example, the individuals on your team are more than quota makers with legs. John C. Maxwell couldn't phrase it any more clearly when he says:

"People don't care how much you know, until they know how much you care."

Find the time to make a genuine effort to discover what is important about the lives of the members of your team **outside** of your organization. One of the most successful leaders I ever worked with was tasked with holding a three-day sales strategy meeting every quarter. Believe me when I say that, thanks to marketing departments and national *leadership*, there were more than enough items to fill a three-day agenda. Despite that, he started every meeting by having all ten members of his team take turns highlighting what was happening in their personal lives that they wanted to share to the group. I can assure you that everyone on the team started the work session on task after having the chance to talk about themselves and their families at the outset.

L.E.A.D., FOLLOW OR
GET OUT OF THE WAY

Youth athletics and amateur golf. There is an interesting common bond between the two. In both cases, the powers that be would like the participants to demonstrate and accomplish something. Unfortunately, those "powers" rarely provide the coaching required for a novice to learn how to learn to do what is being asked. In youth sports the guidance of "Be a good sport!" is a line published in every organizational handbook and uttered at the beginning and completion of every game. Unfortunately, the behaviors that would reflect the trait of good sportsmanship are rarely discussed in detail with the players. Perhaps the players could learn from the behavior modeled by the spectators sitting in the stands. Hmm. I guess there are many times that certainly isn't a good idea. Similarly, were every starter at every golf course given one wish, I am quite certain it would be: "Maintain the pace of play! Stay up with the group in front of you, not ahead of the group behind you!" These are reasonable requests, but if you are one of the multitudes of recreational golfers in America, the demand doesn't do much if you don't know the specific techniques of maintaining pace of play.

Inspirational leaders refuse to fall into that trap. While I can encourage recognition and constructive adjustment as the two most effective methods of developing your people (and thus becoming "The Answer to the Question"), it will do little good if you don't know how to provide feedback so specific behavior is either reinforced or adjusted.

Acronyms are entertaining little tools, once you come up with letters that apply to your concepts and are then able to sequence them to form a word. Prior to the development of an acronym, I believe it takes a crossed wire someplace upstairs to enjoy that task. Thankfully, I possess that crossed wire, and have created what I feel is the perfect acronym for the required elements of positive reinforcement or recognition, as well as constructive adjustment. That acronym is **L.E.A.D.**

As I deconstruct **L.E.A.D.** I feel that it would be helpful to provide examples. Appendices A and B are transcripts of the official citations issued to Colonel John W. Ripley, USMC and Corporal Dakota Meyer, USMC which detailed their actions not in *leadership* situations, but above and beyond the call of duty in the area of *commitment*. As a result, they were awarded our nation's highest military honors. As we explore the concept of **L.E.A.D.**, I won't use those citations as examples of how to **L.E.A.D.** appropriately.

A third citation in Appendix C also relates to a military award. This one was issued not for superhuman efforts but for excellence demonstrated in performing an assigned task, and it provides a helpful example of the **L.E.A.D.** process. It is one thing to talk about Superman and his superpowers, but that doesn't really relate to many of us. As leaders, if we reserve our praise for superhuman efforts, we miss countless opportunities to recognize a job well done. Conversely, if we withhold constructive adjustment for actions resulting in major disasters, we lose the opportunity to develop our people.

Appendix C presents the citation for the U.S. Navy Achievement Medal issued to a Petty Officer 2nd

Class who served as a quartermaster in the U.S. Navy. While her duties took place during wartime, her accomplishments were not the stuff of war stories or movies and would not be considered above the call of duty. She was simply doing her job to the best of her ability. Had she not performed her navigational duties well, her ship may have ended up on a reef, which is the case for most of us, figuratively speaking. If we do our job well, we come back to work tomorrow. If we mess up, disasters of "near biblical proportions" have the possibility of befalling us. (Is that a little melodramatic? Not if the disaster happens to you!) That doesn't mean that if someone does their job well, as you expect them to, they are not worthy of recognition. Remember the concept of reinforcing desired behavior? Doing a job well qualifies as desired behavior. It also doesn't mean we save constructive adjustment for near nuclear meltdowns or praise for leaping tall buildings in a single bound.

With that said, let's execute this deconstruction of the **L.E.A.D.** principle:

L = LINEAR

Every organization needs to have a chain of command with the working relationships spelled out clearly and understandably. As a leader, you will relate to your team members by a virtual straight line. That line may pass through intermediate levels of *leadership* as well. For example, a regional sales manager may have a level of several district sales managers between her and her front-line sales people. In addition, just as your team has a set of leaders, you will as well. On the table of organization, you will be connected to them with the same virtual line. As a team leader, you may also have peers who are also team leaders. Those colleagues may report to the same boss as do you. These are the linear relationships that matter and are addressed here.

The linear relationship demonstrated in our example in Appendix C is represented as follows: The Navy Achievement Medal earned by QM2 Brown was authorized by the Secretary of the Navy. Though it is possible, it is very unlikely that the SecNav personally observed QM2 Brown aboard her ship carrying out her duties at the navigation table in an exemplary manner. Instead, QM2 Brown's leaders were the ones responsible for the issuance of this medal by taking several linear *leadership* steps:

1. They took the time to observe.

QM2 Brown's leaders had their own tasks to accomplish on the bridge of the ship while she was doing her job. Nevertheless, someone (in this case the navigation officer) took the time to observe her performance. The young lieutenant affectionately referred to as "Nav" noticed how well she worked and cared enough to write up an official request for this award.

2. **They made it public.**

   Once her performance was observed, it was then directed linearly up the chain of command. Eventually, word of QM2 Brown's effectiveness made it through several steps from her immediate supervisor to the desk of the Secretary of the Navy.

3. **They made it even more public.**

   Upon approval by the Secretary of the Navy, the citation and award were then returned in a linear fashion back down the chain of command rather than sending it directly to QM2 Brown. Having been signed by the Secretary the Navy (ironically on QM2's father's birthday), it was forwarded back to the Commanding Officer of her ship for a public presentation attended by her shipmates and leaders. The news of the award was also disseminated to her peers through the ship's website and newsletter.

   In this example, we have traced the linear relationship of a situation worthy of praise and recognition. Simply put, when one of your people does something praiseworthy; tell as many people as you can! By all means, follow the lines of the table of organization, but don't stop there! You certainly want to recognize your superstar and make him or her aware of the achievement. You also want to encourage others by sharing the good news with colleagues.

A similar relationship exists if a constructive adjustment is required; it is just not as widespread. A leader who observes the need to adjust the performance of a member of the team should deal with that individual directly and in private whenever possible. This is <u>not</u> a task to be delegated nor publicized beyond the chain of command. If there are intermediate levels of *leadership* between the observing leader and the individual whose behavior is in need of adjustment, all levels between the observer and the offender should be involved in the adjustment process.

As a final step, should your boss be aware of and / or involved in an adjustment situation with one of your people, it is your responsibility to keep that senior leader appraised when the adjustment has been successful. Without your follow up, your boss may labor under the false impression that the individual involved still requires that adjustment, when in fact it may have been mastered in exemplary fashion.

The possibility exists that unacceptable behavior might take place by a teammate in front of the entire team. The temptation to make an example of the offender in front of their peers is understandable, yet it must be tempered. Let me paint the following example:

You have scheduled a meeting at 8:00 a.m. to address a significant issue that involves your entire team.

One member of your team, Shelly, arrives thirty minutes late. There was no notice from Shelly that she would be late. As she casually enters the room, she pulls up a chair with no apology for her tardiness. In fact, her arrival interrupts you and she offers no apology. Her attitude is lackadaisical and she borders on being disrespectful as she takes her seat. Shortly after the room settles, Shelly begins a side conversation generating laughter from her colleagues on either side, again interrupting you.

In a situation like that, this Marine can certainly relate to a desire to read "the riot act" to Shelly in front of the team in order that they all receive the message that her behavior is unacceptable. It may have been tempting, but it also would have been inappropriate and unnecessary. It would suffice to say, "I get the sense that we should take fifteen minutes for a bio break. Shelly, let me see you before <u>your</u> break." I assure you the rest of the team would have gotten the message <u>without</u> you having to violate the public vs. private philosophy.

Shelly's behavior may have been very irritating to you as her leader, but there is one thing that you must remember. You have none of the facts behind her behavior. Addressing the problem that you see is not your first step. It is important that you take the time to talk to Shelly, listen to her and find out what events have conspired to cause her to act in this way. It is possible that she is responding to a personal catastrophe in her own life. Possibly there is a misunderstanding of something that <u>you</u> have done, and she is simply lashing out. While the behavior is inappropriate in any case, it is important that you discover its etiology before applying an incorrect cure. Obviously, a one on one conversation in private is the most effective way for you to get on the same page as Shelly.

From time to time it may be useful to address the behavior in need of adjustment of one individual to other members of the team to provide a learning point. In that event, it is important that the example be sanitized with nothing included that could identify the culprit to the remainder of the team. Nothing is served by correcting one of your teammates in front of their peers, even in a case such as this. Consider using such an example carefully. It is possible that even relating the details of the offense may identify the offender. If that is the case, pass on the opportunity. Find a better way to provide the teaching point. If you can, you would have achieved a spectacular example of focusing on the welfare of your people as well as keeping your mission in mind.

E = EXPLICIT

Despite its gender inappropriateness, I use the term "Atta boy" to symbolize praise. Consider that shorthand for the sake of expedience. Whether it be praise or adjustment, it is mandatory that you be **explicit** in describing the details of behavior. "Atta boy, Bob!" is simply not enough. In examining the events in the appendices, you will find the citations for each of the awards describes in detail what the awardees did to merit recognition. In the example of QM2 Brown it is stated as:

"She planned over 14,000 nautical miles of navigational tracks throughout the Atlantic Ocean and the Mediterranean Sea. She planned, briefed and executed over 30 restricted transits, six straight transits and seven precision anchorages. She trained 13 junior officers in

navigation, helping six officers qualify officer of the deck."

The only way the Navy could have been more explicit in recognizing QM2 Brown's accomplishments would have been to list the longitude and latitude of the navigational events cited and the names of those she trained! The important facet of **leadership** that applies in this example is that one of her leaders had to care enough to pay attention to what she was doing. It is easy to notice when one of your young captains has blown up a bridge to stop an enemy offensive, or that a young corporal braved withering enemy fire time and time again to save his comrades. Her leaders went a step further and watched her do her day to day job.

As a leader with the minimum level of desire to develop others, it is easy to notice the victories of your top tier as well as the challenges faced by your bottom tier. The true leader who cares is also paying attention to that teammate in the middle of the pack, or the **backbone**. This is the individual who used to get Bs and Cs on tests, but is now getting all Bs. It is just as important to be cognizant of the fact that a middle of the packer has been hitting .285 all season and lately his average has been dropping to what now stands at .255.

Being explicit is even more important when you are dealing with a constructive adjustment. Your goal here is not to broadcast a victory to the world to stimulate similar behavior from others as it is with praise and recognition. With a constructive adjustment, you are attempting to correct a behavior that is inappropriate for any of a dozen reasons. Without attempting to adjust that behavior to something acceptable, you are shirking one of your primary tasks as a leader. You are also putting your team's ability to accomplish its mission in jeopardy. In addition, you are neglecting the possibility of developing your people. Be able to specifically discuss the behavior that needs to be changed and what it will look like when it has been changed explicitly.

A = ACCENTUATE THE POSITIVE

There is a special place for this factor in the hearts and minds of all of us. The human animal is naturally defensive. We even have a catch phrase for our response to stress called **Flight or Fight**. Neither taking flight nor fighting provides physiological responses that favor self analysis or calm rational thought. When you call someone into your office or draw attention to them in front of their peers, the mind begins to respond to a perceived threat. In the case of praise and recognition, it is important to set a friendly tone early to put a stop to a surge of adrenaline which is inevitable yet rarely comforting. Since the occasion is a positive one, the last thing you want to do is start it off with a negative perception.

When the situation arises that calls for a corrective adjustment, it becomes even more important to recognize the Fight or Flight phenomena and to temper it. I call this the **Oreo Cookie** principle. I have always considered this initial phase analogous to "giving them a cookie". That way, the label "**The Oreo Cookie Principle**" makes some degree of sense. An Oreo Cooke consists of two chocolate wafers sandwiching a cream center. (I'm sure you are familiar with the cookie to which I refer. You may even have had arguments about the best way to eat one!) With a situation calling for a corrective adjustment, picture this cookie and it will help guide you through the process to make your session as productive and as painless as possible.

Listening to our leader address something we may have done wrong can be a difficult thing for any of us. As a result, all leaders should anticipate this. Attempt to start any corrective adjustments by accentuating the positives of something that your audience brings to your team. We like to call this phase **give them a cookie**. Use this opportunity to remind them of their strengths and the benefits your team realizes because of their positive contributions. (This will become a very important ingredient for the second cookie!)

Now that you have your charge feeling a little better about your one on one meeting, it is time to address explicitly the issue which needs to be adjusted. Focus on the behavior itself and not the individual.

Imagine that you are speaking with someone in your top tier who has uncharacteristically fallen on their sword. Their normal **water walker** status is irrelevant if they have engaged in behavior that has hurt your team. Address the **specific behavior** that needs adjustment and not the personality of the offender.

Conversely, it is very possible this is not the first time the individual in front of you has come up a little bit short and your patience with them may be running just a teensy bit thin. Take a deep breath and count to ten. Make sure you have all the facts in front of you. Once you both have addressed and understand the facts of the situation, focus on the **specific behavior** that is at fault. It is very possible this pattern of behavior is the result of a larger issue. In this case, while the situation may be suitable for discussion, it is not the intended focus of this meeting. The tacky term for this phase is called **cream them** because it is sandwiched between 2 cookies, and is the most important part of this discussion. (Admit it! You don't eat Oreo's for the cookies. It's all about the creamy center! Have I overworked the Oreo Cookie analogy yet? Bear with me. I have 1 more step to go.)

Now it is time to close your discussion with the second cookie. You have just had a heart to heart with one of the people you are responsible for. While it may not have been all grins and giggles for you, it certainly was even less enjoyable for them. No one expects it to be easy for either of you. If you can remember <u>this</u> is how you help people improve and develop, it will improve your outlook. Now it is time to **serve another cookie** by addressing some of the positives they bring to the team. Conclude by explaining how making this adjustment will allow them to help the team and themselves to an even greater degree.

Now that we have tackled the icky part, let us examine how the citation in the appendix accentuates the positive with the concept of praise and recognition. In a different way from being <u>explicit</u> about the behavior, this phase is meant to cite what that behavior has meant to the team and her own self worth. Referring again to the citation to QM2 Brown, she:

"...was a vital member of the Gonzalez navigation team during a standing NATO

Maritime Group Two Deployment. Petty Officer Brown's exceptional professionalism, unrelenting perseverance, and loyal devotion to duty reflected credit upon her and were in keeping with the highest traditions of the United States Naval Service."

Simply put, whether praising or adjusting, <u>explicitly</u> relate the behavior and then draw the line to what it was that the behavior contributed to the team, or could contribute once it is corrected. Keep the focus on the <u>mission</u> and keep the end in mind.

D=DEVELOP

As discussed previously, leaders and even managers that we have all encountered have succeeded in getting their teams to accomplish what needed to be done

Unfortunately, in most cases we can't even remember their names. A select few not only accomplished their mission with their team, but made members of that team more proficient at the same time. That is because they cared enough to spend the extra time required to develop their people.

With the three preceding principles of **commitment, trust** and **caring** in mind, you will be able to provide *leadership* to your team. You can make them aware of what they do well now and improve what they can do better. It is this willingness to develop others and to prepare them for increasing responsibility that will make you "The Answer to the Question." Your efforts to develop your people will bring your name immediately to mind at some random cocktail party decades in the future as I am trying to wrestle a bacon wrapped scallop. Thank you! I love bacon wrapped scallops!

WOMEN IN *LEADERSHIP*: *CARING*

For a woman in a *leadership* role, one could say that addressing the concept of *caring* may be a case of belaboring the obvious. The roles women serve as mothers, caregivers and wives (to name a few) provide ample evidence of the *caring* nature possessed by many. It is my fervent belief that women can master all the capabilities for *leadership* that men may possess. I also believe that some women can have additional strength which can stand them in excellent stead as leaders. *Caring*, without a doubt, can be one of those strengths.

No, I do not propose that women always make better leaders than men. Nor do I believe that men always make better leaders than women. I do believe that one person can be a better leader than another because their behaviors are more in line with effective *leadership* principles. There is no gender distinction here. I also believe the principles I address are the important corner pieces to putting together an effective *leadership* image. No two images will be the same because our experiences and behaviors will all differ. I will propose that the image of *leadership* a woman is constructing may have pieces relating to *caring* that may be easier for her to identify in the mass of remaining pieces. Evidence? In your last office work environment, what gender was the person who was most cognizant of birthday recognition, celebrations of births, weddings and other positive life events. I am willing to bet it was a woman.

It has become apparent to me that life can be a series of tradeoffs. Whenever something good is present, looming around the corner is something not so good. That is a necessary trade off. Perhaps the counterbalance is meant to keep us on our toes. Whatever the reason, the special ability women can have to be *caring* and nurturing individuals carries one of those tradeoffs. As discussed previously, some men seem to be able to be extremely tolerant of being considered a tough boss, or a demanding leader. Unfortunately, many women seem to have a special sensitivity when the same traits that result in those labels for men result in being called the "B" word. It is for this reason that it is critical for all leaders, but especially women, to accept the concept of tough love when leading people.

Should you ever find yourself in a *leadership* circumstance that holds no potential for corrective adjustment, get your resume up to date, because it will inevitably be discovered that your *leadership* position is superfluous and certainly expendable. To paraphrase a classic quote: Leaders, who believe that there is nothing that needs to be done to develop their people, simply don't understand the situation! As a woman and as a leader, apply effort to understand and apply "The Oreo Cookie" principle. Accept this fact. Frequently, what seems overly demanding at the time, in retrospect is the shove that we all need on occasion to realize our potential. Even if the shove results in an overheard "B" word, embrace the fact that they may thank you for it later.

The concept of *caring* about the individuals on your team as people and not just a means to an end has generated a significant level of discussion. A valid point that was made during that discussion is as follows:

"If you are going to use examples of combat *leadership*, you have to be careful about advancing the concept of *caring* about your people as opposed to knowing your people. A combat leader who cares too much may find it difficult to send his troops into harm's way." There is no way that I can argue that fact. A combat leader who finds it easy to send his team into hostile situations is in the wrong job. The source of the thought is a mentor of mine who served in combat and has experienced the anguish of losing men in battle.

Appendix D relates the story of a woman who went above and beyond the call of duty as the wife of an officer who at the same time was leading his men into the first significant engagement of the Vietnam War. That engagement turned out to be a fierce and bloody battle for the Ia Drang Valley in the Republic of Vietnam. Having met both principle characters of the account personally, I can assure you that the level of *caring* that was present for the woman was equivalent to the level of *caring* present in her husband. Recall the guidance that "As a leader, your mission always comes first, but the welfare of your people never comes second." Colonel John Ripley expressed this sentiment as:

"Mission first, Marines always!"

The odds are that you are not going to be leading Marines. Never the less I hope this example will help you understand the concept.

CARING: THE FIRSTSTEP

In the event you read this book in its entirety, you will come close to being able to recite this section by heart. This is just in case only one chapter is deemed pertinent to be read at any one time

We describe the *leadership* relationship as being similar to any personal relationship. The three primary qualities of a leader, *commitment*, *trust* and finally *caring* for your team as individuals are vital to any relationship. They are critical in a romantic relationship, a family relationship, a sales relationship and a platonic relationship. When all three are present, the relationship is at its peak. Remove one element, and the relationship can still function, just not at as high of a level. Remove two elements and the relationship is at serious risk of failure.

The *leadership* relationship is unique in that it requires a leader. In all cases regarding the three qualities I identified, it is up to the leader to **take the first step**. As their leader, you have the benefit of information your teammates do not have. When you bring on new team members, you have the responsibility of ensuring they know what is expected of them. That may mean covering it more than once, in more than one fashion. Communication is a command responsibility. It is simply not acceptable for any of your teammates to ever say with sincerity,

"I had no idea that was expected of me." It's understood that people can use that excuse to shirk responsibility. But if a lack of communication is what caused the shortfall, the responsibility falls directly upon the leader.

Remember, "People don't care how much you know, until they know how much you care." It is repeated here because it is a critical first step when you assume the *leadership* of a team. I can assure you that in those hectic first days, weeks and months, life will be overwhelming with tasks that need to be accomplished. This is true even if your new position does not require the additional burden of relocation. Don't let those important details detract you from the critical task of taking the first step in getting to know your team as people.

That first step might be best taken by letting them get to know you. At your first get together, allow yourself to open up, so your team can see the person who is going to have a huge role in determining their quality of life as long as you are together. Present yourself as the leader following Rule 13: When placed in command, take charge. Follow that up with Rule 14: Do the right thing. Specifically, do the right thing by letting your people get to know you as a real person with feelings, dreams and passion. Once you have opened up to them, they will find it much easier to

Become THE LEADER Your PEOPLE DESERVE

open up to you.

173

RICHARD BROWN

THE LEADERSHIP SPOTLIGHT

"It is not the honor that you take with you but the heritage you leave behind."

--Branch Rickey

RICHARD BROWN

THE LEADERSHIP SPOTLIGHT

On an annual basis, the high school sports associations in many states conduct Spirit Championships. On one weekend in December, athletes from every high school in our state compete with other schools in their respective divisions for the crown of State Cheer or Dance Champions. Trust me when I say that attending this event makes for a very special day! The championships are twelve hours full of perky energy, drama and tears. While it is true that the mind can only retain what the butt can endure, the heart has a capacity all its own.

As one might expect, after the day's competition there is an award ceremony. All the teams that have earned the honor to compete in the final round of competition return to the arena floor and sit together as teams. Their coaches stand off to the side, chatting nervously with each other or waiting in pained anticipatory silence with their assistants. For a visitor, there is no visible way of identifying the coaches of the various teams unless you know them personally. For twenty or thirty stress filled minutes, everyone present attempts to keep their own butterflies flying in some sort of formation in their stomach, some more successfully than others. While the final scores are confirmed by the judges, the participants wait for the winners to be crowned.

Eventually, the moment of truth arrives. All the athletes from each team (sans coaches) sit in a circle in the middle of the arena floor clutching the hands of their teammates. Their heads are bowed and their eyes are squeezed tightly shut. You can almost hear the silent prayers to whatever powers are relevant echoing off the coliseum rafters. Only the second place and championship awards are announced from a field of half a dozen or so teams that were selected to compete in the finals.

After the announcement of the second-place team, two events take place in rapid succession. The second-place team is rightfully pleased with their performance, and it shows in their reaction. Second place is nothing to be ashamed of, but their exultation is tempered by the fact that some other squad will be named champion. The remaining teams squeeze their eyes shut a little tighter. The silent pleading becomes significantly louder (irony intended) and after the requisite dramatic pause from the announcer, that year's state spirit champion is named. I

It is difficult to believe the celebration that follows has yet to seriously injure any of the participants. Initially the athletes spring to an altitude between twelve and eighteen inches above the mat from a sitting position, amazingly without the soles of their shoes touching the mat. Tears, hugs and sobs dominate the next thirty seconds, until the announcer is obliged to remind the team to come to center mat so they may receive their trophy.

It is obvious that to these champions the hardware is merely a symbol and thus an afterthought. The team has sweat, bled, cried and fought for eight months to reach this moment. They are State Champions! Any drama that may have existed between them has vanished as their school name echoes through the building. Eventually they do make their way to center mat and hoist the trophy over their heads.

One school in our state has been particularly successful in racking up state titles. It is obvious that the Coach has skills that allow her to create champions. *On the occasion that her squad lifts the coveted trophy, her name automatically comes to mind with the thought "Wow! She put another great team on the floor!"*

Unfortunately, the awe of her team-building ability diminishes before her squad has had the opportunity to stop crying with joy. Somehow, within seconds of the trophy being received by the team captain from the official, the Coach has transformed herself from one of the anonymous individuals at the periphery of the celebration. In "The Leadership Spotlight", she becomes the center of attention to all and not in a particularly favorable way. Immediately, the trophy finds its way out of the team's hands and into her hands as she runs around the coliseum, trophy extended above her head at arm's length, with her team following behind. In one single instant, this Coach has obliterated most of the respect she earned due to the performance of her squad. During her victory lap, it is all about her. She appears to be someone who has forgotten why she is there. Apparently, the talent of those on her team has somehow made up for her leadership deficiencies. Imagine what they could achieve under different leadership techniques.

In "The Foundations of *Leadership*" section of this book, while addressing the rewards of being a leader, I referred to a concept as "The *Leadership* Spotlight." This concept is important enough to be designated as the final corner piece of the *leadership* puzzle. Without a full understanding of its characteristics, it won't matter if you have completely mastered the concepts of *trust*, *caring* and *commitment*. The phenomenon of "The *Leadership* Spotlight" takes place immediately upon being designated as a leader. It gains added significance the moment you are introduced to your team as their leader. It is critical that you appreciate its existence to keep yourself out of the bad side of any of an infinite number of situations. These instances can create doubt about your very ability to lead.

"The *Leadership* Spotlight" is an opportunity, or a potential pitfall, that all leaders have in common. It doesn't matter if you are a senior executive or a first line supervisor. You could be the president of a sorority or a squad leader in the Marine Corps infantry. Regardless of your mission or the size of your team, you can expect to frequently deal with the same interesting phenomenon best described as "The *Leadership* Spotlight."

Imagine your presence in a room full of your teammates. The room is brightly lit and to the casual observer entering the room it would be difficult if not impossible to immediately identify you as the leader of the group. For the purposes of this analogy you should be aware that when you accepted your current *leadership* position, an intensely powerful yet virtual spotlight was directed upon you. The spotlight follows your every move. Because of the ambient illumination in the room, the light from the spotlight is barely noticeable to those around you most of the time.

Should the room lights ever be turned off by circumstances, the spotlight will remain on and you will be the only person in the room illuminated by "The *Leadership* Spotlight." Everyone's attention will be directed at you. Your every move will be evident to all. Welcome to *leadership*! Regardless of the locale, position or industry, the principle of "The *Leadership* Spotlight" will be ready to illuminate your actions wherever you go. Life coach Tony Robbins has said that "In moments of decision, your destiny is determined." The principle of "The *Leadership* Spotlight" brings life to that philosophy.

There are some interesting phenomena that happen when you are illuminated by this spotlight. You may be the leader of the entire group, but only occasionally will you have the ability to control the ambient light that makes the spotlight almost disappear. In fact, it is almost as if a mischievous little gremlin has control of the room lights. That obnoxious creature will, from time to time, let a warped sense of humor influence its actions. On occasion, you may get the gremlin to cooperate with your wishes. There may even be times when you can influence the level of ambient illumination. Usually, however, your gremlin will douse the room lights at exactly the wrong time, with no warning whatsoever.

You now have been able to find and place three of the four corner pieces of your *leadership* puzzle. Internalizing the principle of "The *Leadership* Spotlight" will allow you to place the fourth corner piece, move on and begin to fill in the remainder of the border as well as the interior to begin to complete your image of *leadership*. We have explored the importance of *trust*, *caring* and *commitment*. The ultimate *leadership* relationship can account for all three of these attributes directing themselves from the leader to the team and from the team to the leader. Whenever the word chemistry is used to describe a sports team, this is what they are referring to.

As a leader, it is imperative that whenever you find yourself in "The *Leadership* Spotlight", you are behaving in concert with the principles of *trust*, *caring* and *commitment*. To be seen acting in an untrustworthy, uncaring or uncommitted manner can do serious damage to your image in the eyes of your team. Depending on the severity of the transgression, it has the potential to destroy your ability to lead with no hope of recovery. Don't let that happen! In a more positive light (pun intended) a demonstration of *trust*, *caring* or *commitment* as the situation warrants when you are illuminated in these moments of decision can go a long way towards enhancing the morale of your team and reinforcing your image as an effective and inspiring leader. These are the moments that, accumulated over the course of a relationship between the leader and their team, contribute significantly to the selection of your name as the answer to the question at the cocktail party.

To display your ability as a leader, make sure you behave as a leader whenever you are thrust into the spotlight. Seems simple enough, right? Oh, wait! There is that little matter of the fact that you have little or no control over when those moments are going to occur. With that in mind, does that mean you need to sharpen your response time? When you find yourself in that *leadership* defining moment do you need lightning fast reactions to succeed? Absolutely not! When the light comes on, you are being evaluated as a leader before your eyes can even begin to adjust to the glare. Trying to anticipate the spotlight is like reacting to a speed trap by stepping on the brakes to bring your speed under the posted limit. Usually you are too late. By the time you see the officer pointing the radar gun in your direction; they have your speed already recorded and they are on your tail, lights blazing and siren wailing.

The key to ensuring that you are perceived as a leader in your moments of decision is where Rule 14 comes into play. Remember "Do the right thing"? That is always the key to success! Assume your command, and from that moment on, make the commitment to yourself to always "Do the right thing." Reverting to our speed trap analogy: If you don't want to get caught exceeding the speed limit in a speed trap - simply don't speed! If you don't want to find yourself behaving poorly in a *leadership* situation - then don't behave poorly! Make it a rule to always do the right thing, and always choose the hard right vs. the easy wrong. Follow this advice and your gremlin will become your best friend.

There is a very important caveat to the whole *leadership* spotlight philosophy. If moments of decision determine our destiny, you may have to fight the temptation to hasten the occurrence of those opportunities. Remember the Coach at the state championships? That would be an example of someone hoping that the room lights will go out so she is the center of attention. Individuals who have this type of mindset see the logic that says: "If I start a fire and if I am seen putting it out, I will be cast as a hero." Do yourself and your team a favor and keep your hand off the light switch! The best you can hope for is to be able to anticipate the switch being thrown.

The first time you address your team is a perfect example of an anticipated opportunity to lead. In a situation such as that, you know the spotlight will be on you. After all, this is your gremlin's first chance at mischief since the last *leadership* position you held. If this is your first experience with *leadership*, your gremlin has been trembling with anticipation. As your puzzle begins to fill in, experience will bring new tools to you and hone your skills. All it takes is one speeding ticket through a school zone at 3:00 p.m. on a school day to help you anticipate the presence of a policeman being there the next time you cruise through at thirty-five m.p.h. during the same time of day. As you accumulate and join more and more puzzle pieces, those opportunities will be easier for you to anticipate.

AND SO, IT BEGINS

*"Use power to help people. For we are given
power not to advance our own purposes,
not to make a great show in the world, nor a name.
There is but one just use of power
and it is to serve people."*

--George H.W. Bush

RICHARD BROWN

AND SO, IT BEGINS

So here we are, at the beginning of what hopefully is a *leadership* experience that helps define your career in a way that is worthy of your legacy. Your foundation is in place. You have found and placed the four corner pieces of the puzzle to begin the formation of your own image of *leadership*. We have explored the importance of *commitment*, *trust* and *caring* as necessary foci for the effective and inspirational leader. By adopting those qualities as the core values that drive your decisions and your actions, you can operate with confidence when "The *Leadership* Spotlight" dominates and you become the center of attention. In that case, you can rest easy that your behavior will be appropriate for your leadership role. As a result, you are well on your way to becoming the leader your people deserve.

You still have a bit of work remaining however. Off to the side, within your reach, is a pile of puzzle pieces that all contribute to your *leadership* image. Those pieces are not going to jump into the appropriate place in the puzzle by themselves. For the image to form, you must actively seek out the proper pieces. The printed sides are all facing up, but that is the only level of organization that exists with their arrangement. As you encounter day to day decisions, challenges and opportunities you will, in effect, be reaching for a puzzle piece that you hope to be able to join to those that have preceded it. Sometimes that choice will be the one which you seek. At other times, after considerable examination, that piece will need to be placed aside for use later. It is important to remember that even if it isn't a good fit right now, that piece will eventually fill a spot in your image.

As the empty space begins to fill in with an identifiable scene, remember that every piece will be directly or indirectly linked to the four initial corner pieces of **commitment**, **trust**, **caring** and "The **Leadership** Spotlight." As you encounter the **leadership** experiences of others as well as your own, I challenge you to find the linkage between that specific piece of the puzzle and at least one of the four initial corner pieces. I assure you, if you look hard enough, you will find that any specific example of effective and inspirational **leadership** is linked to the major qualities discussed in this book.

I have attempted to reinforce my various philosophies with examples of stories from real life. In those instances, they were selected to focus on one specific trait or principle. I will leave you with one final example. Appendix E relates the behavior of a combat leader during the Korean conflict. Read the account with a wide focus and I am certain that you will be able to see the role played by the principles of *commitment*, *trust* and *caring* when the actions of the enemy placed the American Commander squarely in "The *Leadership* Spotlight".

As I discussed in the opening, it is my fervent hope that this book will prove to be a useful contribution to your personal development. I hope that these stories and opinions (as well as the random tangents) will help you become not just a leader who gets the job done, but truly the leader your people deserve. It is certainly true that a *leadership* position very likely will be challenging, fatiguing, confounding and frustrating experience at times. Just as true, the rewards that come from positively influencing the life of another individual through *commitment*, *trust* and *caring* for even a short period can provide sufficient rewards to your own life to make the experience worthwhile...and then some. It is unrealistic to expect to enrich the lives of everyone you lead and for you to become "The Answer to the Question" for all. However, the knowledge that you have changed the lives of even a handful of them can

RICHARD BROWN

make the sacrifices required of **_leadership_** worthwhile.

APPENDIX A[4]

The President of the United States in the name of
the Congress takes pleasure in presenting the

NAVY CROSS
to
CAPTAIN JOHN W. RIPLEY
UNITED STATES MARINE CORPS

The President of the United States of America
takes pleasure in presenting the Navy Cross to
Captain John W. Ripley (MCSN: 0-84239), United
States Marine Corps, for extraordinary heroism on 2
April 1972 while serving as the Senior Marine Advisor
to the Third Vietnamese Marine Corps Infantry
Battalion in the Republic of Vietnam. Upon receipt of
a report that a rapidly moving, mechanized, North
Vietnamese army force, estimated at reinforced
divisional strength, was attacking south along Route
#1, the Third Vietnamese Marine Infantry Battalion
was positioned to defend a key village and the
surrounding area. It became imperative that a vital
river bridge be destroyed if the overall security of the

---

[4] www.freerepublic.com/fuxus.news/28668/replies?c=83

northern provinces of Military Region One was to be maintained. Advancing to the bridge to personally supervise this most dangerous but vitally important assignment, Captain Ripley located a large amount of explosives which had been pre-positioned there earlier, access to which was blocked by a chain-link fence. In order to reposition the approximately 500 pounds of explosives, Captain Ripley was obliged to reach up and hand-walk along the beams while his body dangled beneath the bridge. On five separate occasions, in the face of constant enemy fire, he moved to points along the bridge and, with the aid of another advisor who pushed the explosives to him, securely emplaced them. He then detonated the charges and destroyed the bridge, thereby stopping the enemy assault. By his heroic actions and extraordinary courage, Captain Ripley undoubtedly was instrumental in saving an untold number of lives. His inspiring efforts reflected great credit upon himself, the Marine Corps, and the United States Naval Service.

APPENDIX B[5]

The President of the United States in the name of
the Congress takes pleasure in presenting the

MEDAL OF HONOR
to
CORPORAL DAKOTA L. MEYER
UNITED STATES MARINE CORPS

For service as set forth in the following:

For conspicuous gallantry and intrepidity at the
repeated risk of his life above and beyond the call of
duty as a member of Marine Embedded Training
Team 2-8, Regional Corps Advisory Command 3-7, in
Kunar Province, Afghanistan, on 8 September 2009.
When the forward element of his combat team began
to be hit by intense fire from roughly 50 Taliban
insurgents dug-in and concealed on the slopes above
Ganjgal village, Corporal Meyer mounted a gun-truck,
enlisted a fellow Marine to drive, and raced to attack
the ambushers and aid the trapped Marines and
Afghan soldiers. During a six hour fire fight, Corporal

---

[5] http://projects.militarytimes.com/citations-medals-
awards/recipient.php?recipient id=3957

Meyer single-handedly turned the tide of the battle, saved 36 Marines and soldiers and recovered the bodies of his fallen brothers. Four separate times he fought the kilometer up into the heart of a deadly U-shaped ambush. During the fight, he killed at least eight Taliban, personally evacuated 12 friendly wounded, and provided cover for another 24 Marines and soldiers to escape likely death at the hands of a numerically superior and determined foe. On his first foray his lone vehicle drew machine gun, mortar, rocket grenade and small arms fire while he rescued five wounded soldiers. His second attack disrupted the enemy's ambush and he evacuated four more wounded Marines. Switching to another gun-truck because his was too damaged they again sped in for a third time, and as turret gunner killed several Taliban attackers at point blank range and suppressed enemy fire so 24 Marines and soldiers could break-out. Despite being wounded, he made a fourth attack with three others to search for missing team members. Nearly surrounded and under heavy fire he dismounted the vehicle and searched house to house to recover the bodies of his fallen team members. By his extraordinary heroism, presence of mind amidst chaos and death, and unselfish devotion to his comrades in the face of great danger, Corporal Meyer reflected great credit upon himself and upheld the highest traditions of the Marine Corps and the United States Naval Service.

RICHARD BROWN

APPENDIX C[6]

DEPARTMENT OF THE NAVY

THIS IS TO CERTIFY THAT
THE SECRETARY OF THE NAVY HAS
AWARDED THE
NAVY AND MARINE CORPS
ACHIEVEMENT MEDAL
to
QUARTERMASTER SECOND CLASS
(SURFACE WARFARE/AIR WARFARE)
PAULA BROWN,
UNITED STATES NAVY

For professional achievement in the performance of her duties as Chart Petty Officer in USS GONZALEZ (DDG 66) from February 2008 through August 2008. Petty Officer Brown was a vital member of the Gonzalez Navigation team during a standing NATO Maritime Group Two deployment. She planned over 14,000 nautical miles of navigational tracks throughout the Atlantic Ocean and the Mediterranean Sea. She planned, briefed and executed over 30 restricted transits, six strait transits and seven

---

precision anchorages. She trained 13 junior officers in navigation, helping six officers qualify officer of the deck. Petty Officer Brown's exceptional professionalism, unrelenting perseverance, and loyal devotion to duty reflected credit upon her and were in keeping with the highest traditions of the United States Naval Service.

APPENDIX D[7]

She may not have been a soldier, but Julie Moore is buried in the midst of them. An Army daughter, wife and mother, she worked tirelessly to change the way the Army notified families of war fatalities.

Julie's husband, LTC Hal Moore (later LTG Moore), commanded the 1st Battalion, 7th Cavalry, in the battle of the Ia Drang Valley in Vietnam. It was the first major battle for American troops in Vietnam, lasted 3 days and saw numerous fatalities. Living at Fort Benning, Julie's heart stopped when she saw a taxi driver at her front door. She learned he was not handing over a notice of her husband's death, but was trying to find the address of another wife, whose husband had died in the battle. She followed him to the new widow's house and took it upon herself to be with and support the women who learned their husbands had been killed in action.

Horrified by the way the Army handled death notifications; she decided to challenge the policy. Within just two weeks, the Army began sending a chaplain and officer to deliver the news, rather than

[7] NATIONAL INFANTRY MUSEUM & SOLDIER Center http://www.nationalinfantrymuseum.org/31 days-31stories/

just sending a telegram via taxi driver. This was the beginning of a major reorganization by the Army to provide support for families of soldiers. Julie not only saw a problem but she found a compassionate and *caring* solution. Julie's actions are chronicled in the book "We Were Soldiers Once...and Young," co-authored by her husband and news reporter Joe Galloway, and later in the movie "We Were Soldiers." The Julia Compton Moore Award is given annually to civilian spouses of soldiers for "Outstanding Contributions to the United States Army."

When she died in 2004, she left behind her husband and five children. She is buried at Fort Benning near her parents and her husband's soldiers whose families she consoled during those dark days of November 1965.

Julie Moore – she went the extra mile for military families.

APPENDIX E[8]

The President of the United States in the name of the Congress takes pleasure in presenting the

MEDAL OF HONOR
to
CAPTAIN WILLIAM E. BARBER
UNITED STATES MARINE CORPS

For conspicuous gallantry and intrepidity at the risk of his life above and beyond the call of duty as Commanding Officer of Company F, Second Battalion, Seventh Marines, First Marine Division (Reinforced), in action against enemy aggressor forces in Korea from November 28, to December 2, 1950.

Assigned to defend a three-mile mountain pass along the division's main supply line and commanding the only route of approach in the march from Yudam-Ni to Hagaru-ri, Captain Barber took position with his battle-weary troops and, before nightfall, had dug in and set up a defense along the frozen snow-covered hillside. When a force of estimated regimental strength savagely attacked during the night, inflicting heavy casualties and finally surrounding his position

---

[8] www.arlingtoncemeter.net/webarber.htm

following a bitterly fought seven-hour conflict, Captain Barber, after repulsing the enemy, gave assurance that he could hold if supplied by air drops and requested permission to stand fast when orders were received by radio to fight his way back to a relieving force after two reinforcing units had been driven back under fierce resistance in their attempts to reach the isolated troops. Aware that leaving the position would sever contact with the 8,000 Marines trapped at Yudam-ni and jeopardize their chances of joining the 3,000 more awaiting their arrival in Hagaru-ri for the continued drive to the sea, he chose to risk loss of his command rather than sacrifice more men if the enemy seized control and forced a renewed battle to regain the position, or abandon his many wounded who were unable to walk. Although severely wounded in the leg in the early morning of the 29th, Captain Barber continued to maintain personal control, often moving up and down the lines on a stretcher to direct the defense and consistently encouraging and inspiring his men to supreme efforts despite the staggering opposition. Waging desperate battle throughout five days and six nights of repeated onslaughts launched by the fanatical aggressors, he and his heroic command accounted for approximately 1,000 enemy dead in this epic stand in bitter subzero weather, and when the company was relieved only two of his original 220 men were able to walk away from the position so valiantly defended against insuperable odds. His profound faith and courage, great personal valor, and unwavering fortitude were decisive factors in the successful withdrawal of the division from the deathtrap in the Chosin Reservoir sector and reflect the highest credit upon Captain Barber, his intrepid officers and men, and the United States Naval Service.

RICHARD BROWN

About the Author:

Richard Brown

Richard has been putting together his own *leadership* puzzle for his entire adult life. That includes his college years, rarely included in anyone's definition of adult.

As a midshipman enrolled in the Naval ROTC program at Oregon State University, he was one of two selected to serve in a midshipman officer position as a junior. In his senior year, was appointed as Midshipman Battalion Commander, the highest *leadership* position available to a student. Named the USMC Honor Graduate, he served his active duty as an infantry officer with the 1st Marine Brigade in Kaneohe, Hawaii. (It was a dirty job, but somebody had to do it!) Prior to leaving the Corps, Richard was selected ahead of his peers for promotion to captain.

In 1978, he began a 33-year career in sales with Pfizer Inc. Four years later he was one of the youngest individuals at the time promoted to District Manager.

In 2001, Richard returned to the field to apply his experience to the most challenging type of *leadership*, leading his peers.

Richard helped found PRE or Professional Resource Enhancement in 1998 as a means of bringing his unique vision of *leadership* to small businesses, coaches, teachers and young adults. After retiring from Pfizer in 2012, Richard has dedicated his "second adulthood" to exploring, discussing and teaching *leadership* to those that desire to accept that challenge.

www.ingramcontent.com/pod-product-compliance
Lightning Source LLC
Chambersburg PA
CBHW051212170526
45166CB00005B/1863